Meredith Levy

Interactive

Workbook 4 with Downloadable Audio

CAMBRIDGE
UNIVERSITY PRESS

CAMBRIDGE
UNIVERSITY PRESS

University Printing House, Cambridge CB2 8BS, United Kingdom

One Liberty Plaza, 20th Floor, New York, NY 10006, USA

477 Williamstown Road, Port Melbourne, VIC 3207, Australia

314–321, 3rd Floor, Plot 3, Splendor Forum, Jasola District Centre, New Delhi – 110025, India

103 Penang Road, #05-06/07, Visioncrest Commercial, Singapore 238467

Cambridge University Press is part of the University of Cambridge.

It furthers the University's mission by disseminating knowledge in the pursuit of education, learning and research at the highest international levels of excellence.

www.cambridge.org
Information on this title: www.cambridge.org/9780521712255

First published 2012

20 19

Printed in Great Britain by CPI Group (UK) Ltd, Croydon CR0 4YY

A catalogue record for this publication is available from the British Library

ISBN 978-0-521-71225-5 Workbook with Downloadable Audio
ISBN 978-0-521-71224-8 Student's Book with Web Zone access
ISBN 978-0-521-71226-2 Teacher's Book with Web Zone access
ISBN 978-0-521-71227-9 Teacher's Resource Pack
ISBN 978-0-521-71228-6 Class Audio CDs
ISBN 978-0-521-14728-6 DVD (PAL)
ISBN 978-0-521-14729-3 DVD (NTSC)
ISBN 978-0-521-27962-8 Classware DVD-ROM
ISBN 978-0-521-27964-2 Testmaker CD-ROM and Audio CD

Contents

1 Connected

1 Grammar Grammar reference: page 76

Simple and continuous tense review

a Complete the sentences with the correct form of the verbs.

1 They .... (chat) online at the moment.
2 This shop .... (close) at 12:30 on Sundays.
3 I lost my wallet while we .... (walk) home.
4 Jane .... (buy) her phone six months ago.
5 My brother .... (train) to be a doctor now.
6 We .... (not play) this game very often. It's too slow.
7 I .... (not get) your message until yesterday evening.
8 He couldn't see very well because he .... (not wear) his glasses

b Write the questions and match them with the answers.

1 Hi, Linda. Where / you / go?
.... ☐

2 How often / you / send / emails?
.... ☐
....

3 Why / Mike / call / you yesterday?
.... ☐
....

4 Anna / work / today?
.... ☐

5 I saw your brother outside the BBC building. What / he / do / there?
.... ☐

6 it / cost / anything to join the club?
.... ☐
....

7 I tried to ring you a few times last night. you / study?
.... ☐

A No, today's her day off.
B I don't know. He didn't leave a message.
C To the supermarket. I need some new batteries.
D Yes, I was writing my English essay.
E Hardly ever. I prefer chatting online.
F No, it's free.
G His girlfriend works there, so he was probably waiting for her.

c 2 Complete the dialogue with the correct form of the verbs. Then listen and check.

A: What [1] .... you .... (do), Nick?
B: I [2] .... (upload) my photos from Saturday's party. Come and have a look.
A: Hey, that's a great photo of Kate!
B: Yeah. I [3] .... (take) that while she [4] .... (dance) with Sam. They look pretty cool, don't they?
A: I [5] .... (not see) them dancing.
B: No, you [6] .... (talk) to Chris in the other room. There you are, see?
A: Oh no! Why [7] .... I always .... (look) so terrible in photos? Please don't put that one on your Facebook page. I [8] .... (not want) everyone to see me looking like an idiot.
B: OK, I won't! Anyway, it [9] .... (be) a great party, wasn't it?
A: Yeah, I think everyone [10] .... (enjoy) it.

2 Vocabulary

Online communication

a Complete the sentences with the words in the box. There are two extra words.

links digital spam request viral tag settings

1 The video went .... In three days it was viewed by over two million people.
2 I got a friend .... from Nikki's brother and I've added him to my list.
3 Your .... footprint shows all the information about you that can be seen on the web.
4 I .... all my videos so it's easy to see who is in them.
5 The .... on this page take you to other articles by the same author.

b Choose the correct answer: A, B or C.

1 If you defriend someone on your social network site, they
  A can't read your posts on the site.
  B can't find out anything about you on the internet.
  C lose contact with your other friends on the site.
2 When you tag a photo, you
  A download it from the internet.
  B use key words to identify people in it.
  C change the image using digital technology.
3 On a website, you can often find links which
  A allow you to write a comment on the topic.
  B search for information that you want to find.
  C connect you to other web pages.
4 *Spam* is the word for
  A negative comments on social network sites.
  B unwanted messages that are sent to lots of people.
  C products that you can buy online.
5 You use privacy settings on a social network site to
  A increase the number of people who can read your news.
  B reduce the number of people who can read your news.
  C read other people's profiles.
6 If something goes viral on the internet, it
  A is seen by a huge number of people.
  B spreads false information about people.
  C damages people's computer systems.

3 Listen

a 3 Listen to three teenagers talking about social networking. Which question are they answering?

A How do you choose your friends on your social network?
B How do you feel about defriending people?
C What do you do about security on your social network?

b 3 Listen again and write the correct name: Amy, David or Lisa.

1 .... has hundreds of friends.
2 .... is feeling better because he/she defriended someone.
3 .... uses his/her social network to play games.
4 .... and .... had problems with a friend who was posting messages on their site.
5 .... thinks that a future boss might look at his/her site.
6 .... checks his/her friends list regularly.
7 .... decided not to take anyone off his/her friends list.
8 .... knows most of his/her friends personally.

c What are your answers to the questions in Exercise 3a? Prepare to talk about this in your next class.

4 Vocabulary

Phrasal verbs with *up*

a Match the two parts of the sentences.

1 Sara came up ☐
2 Could you turn up ☐
3 They've set up ☐
4 I've built up ☐
5 He gave up ☐
6 Have you charged up ☐
7 I think he made up ☐
8 She looked up ☐

A trying to learn Japanese.
B information on several websites.
C the video camera?
D with a brilliant plan.
E that story.
F a fantastic network of friends.
G the volume?
H a new online shop.

b Complete the crossword.

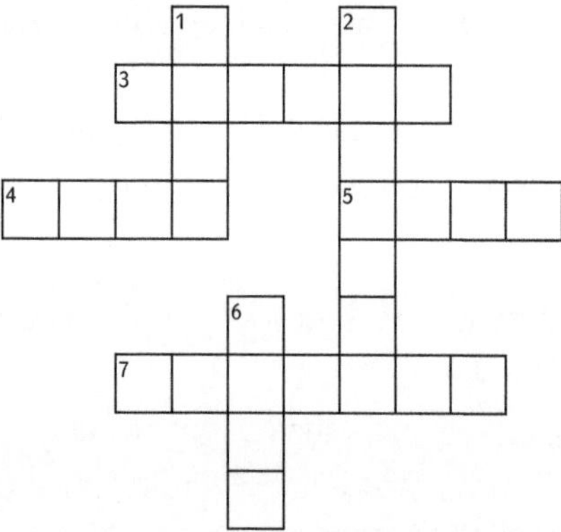

Across

3 I couldn't understand the word, so I .... it up in the dictionary.
4 My father used to smoke, but he .... it up years ago.
5 The music isn't loud enough. Let's .... it up.
7 I've just .... up my phone. The battery was getting low.

Down

1 I'm finding it hard to .... up with a good idea for my Art project.
2 They're .... up their own recording studio now.
6 Nobody could .... up a story like that! It must be true.

Help yourself!

Phrasal verbs for using a computer

Here are three more verbs with *up*. Match them with the definitions.

1 I always **back up** my files by saving them on an external hard disk. ☐
2 When you enter some sites, new windows **pop up** with advertisements. ☐
3 If you **scroll up** to the top of the article, you'll be able to see the title. ☐

A to appear suddenly on the screen
B to make a copy of your material so that you can't lose it
C to move to an earlier part of the page on your screen

Complete these phrasal verbs. Use your dictionary to check.

in off down out

1 To move to a lower part of the page on your screen, you scroll ....
2 When you turn on your machine, it starts working. It stops when you turn it ....
3 On some websites you have to log .... by typing your user name and password.
4 When you want a copy of something on paper, you print it ....

5 Grammar Grammar reference: pages 76 and 78

Perfect tense review

a Read each sentence and then decide if the statement below is *right* (✓) or *wrong* (✗).

1 *I've had a laptop with a touch screen for ages.*
I don't own this computer now. ☐

2 *Since April she's been learning to drive.*
She started learning in April and she's still having lessons. ☐

3 *I've just been searching for information online.*
I'm continuing my search at the moment. ☐

4 *He'd never been to India before.*
It was his first visit to India. ☐

5 *They'd already decided to get a new TV when they saw the advert.*
They made their decision after they saw the advert. ☐

6 *I'd been having a problem with my printer.*
I don't have the problem now, but it lasted for some time. ☐

b Circle the correct words.

1 Omar came half an hour ago with some DVDs for you. *I've / I'd* put them on your desk.
2 Have they *seen / been seeing* this video before?
3 I *haven't / hadn't* heard of this band before I saw them on YouTube.
4 What have you *done / been doing* since I last saw you?
5 When the game ended, we realised we'd *played / been playing* for nearly three hours.
6 Joanna has *read / been reading* that book for three weeks and she still hasn't *finished / been finishing* it!

c Choose the correct answer: A, B or C.

19-year-old Martin Klein has just [1]........ an interesting discovery in the family garage. He was clearing out some rubbish when he found a box containing an old computer, called the Apple Lisa 1. Martin's mother [2]........ the machine in 1984. When she put it in the garage eight years later, it was completely out of date. She had offered it for sale but no one [3]........ it. So when Martin found it last month, it [4]........ sitting in its original box in the garage for about 20 years.

Now, however, people [5]........ collecting unusual early computers and the value of the Lisa 1 [6]........ going up. 'I've [7]........ some research and I think it's worth about $10,000 now,' Martin says. 'We [8]........ decided what to do with it yet, but [9]........ always been interested in computer technology and I'd like to keep it. It's a lovely old machine.'

1 **A** made **B** makes **C** been making
2 **A** has bought **B** had bought **C** had been buying
3 **A** wants **B** had wanted **C** had been wanting
4 **A** is **B** has been **C** had been
5 **A** have started **B** had started **C** had been starting
6 **A** has **B** had **C** has been
7 **A** did **B** been doing **C** had been doing
8 **A** haven't **B** hadn't **C** haven't been
9 **A** I'm **B** I've **C** I'd

6 Pronunciation

/ʃ/, /dʒ/ and /tʃ/

a 4 Tick (✓) the words which have the /dʒ/ sound. Then listen, check and repeat.

jacket	☐	tiger	☐
enjoy	☐	message	☐
finger	☐	together	☐
bridge	☐	energy	☐
digital	☐	angry	☐

b 5 Listen and tick (✓) the word you hear.

	/ʃ/		/tʃ/	
1	sheep	☐	cheap	☐
2	share	☐	chair	☐
3	shoes	☐	choose	☐
4	wish	☐	which	☐
5	cash	☐	catch	☐
6	wash	☐	watch	☐

c 6 Listen and tick (✓) the sound you hear in each word. Then listen again and repeat.

		/ʃ/	/dʒ/	/tʃ/
1	fu<u>t</u>ure	☐	☐	☐
2	connec<u>t</u>ion	☐	☐	☐
3	teena<u>g</u>er	☐	☐	☐
4	a<u>ch</u>ievement	☐	☐	☐
5	expre<u>ss</u>ion	☐	☐	☐
6	langua<u>ge</u>	☐	☐	☐

d 7 Listen and practise saying these phrases.

a chat show — children's pictures
a search engine — a dangerous situation
a huge machine — a challenging question

8 Practise saying these words

charge component frequently privacy
profile reflect research socialise
spread suitable viral visible

7 Read

a Read the text and choose the correct answer: A, B or C.

The article is about

A an invitation that went viral.
B the popularity of social network sites.
C security problems on Facebook.

Most people know how to use social networking sites wisely, but this isn't always the case. In March 2011, Australian teenager Jessica Cooper posted an invitation to her 16th birthday party on Facebook. She was expecting her classmates from school to come and she invited them to bring a few other friends if they wanted to. But she made two big mistakes: she set her private party as a 'public event', and she included her address and mobile phone number in her post. The next day she was horrified to find that around 1,900 people had accepted her invitation and her phone was full of messages from strangers.

Jess quickly removed the invitation, but her problems were just beginning. Someone had already copied her information and almost immediately the event was posted again, using a fake Facebook account in her name. This time it really went viral. By the following morning, 30,000 people had signed up to attend her party and the numbers were increasing every minute. By the time the fake account was shut down by Facebook a day later, more than 200,000 people had accepted the invitation and the event wall was crowded with messages about what they were going to do and bring. Even after the event had been deleted from Facebook, websites and blogs kept making up stories about the party, people were reproducing Jess's profile photo and photos of her house, and businesses were advertising 'Jess Cooper's party' T-shirts for sale.

For lots of people, this was a good joke, but for Jess it wasn't funny. 'I'm so scared,' she told a reporter at the time. Her birthday party, of course, was called off and her parents had to ask the police for protection on the night she had been planning to hold it. She had to close her Facebook and phone accounts, and she probably still feels embarrassed about the unwanted publicity she got in 2011.

b Are the sentences *right* (✓), *wrong* (✗) or *doesn't say* (–)?

1 Jess was 15 when she put her party invitation on Facebook. ☐
2 She hadn't been planning a big public party to celebrate her birthday. ☐
3 Lots of Jess's school friends said they were coming to the party. ☐
4 Jess removed the invitation because someone had copied it. ☐
5 The invitation reappeared on a new account that Jess had set up. ☐
6 Jess's party was still getting lots of attention after the fake account disappeared from Facebook. ☐
7 Jess enjoyed being famous all over the internet. ☐
8 Since this event, Jess has never used a social networking site again. ☐

Portfolio 1

Tell the story of an interesting event connected with a social networking site. It can be about an experience you have had yourself or something you have heard or read about. Use a variety of tenses in your story.

Example topics

- making contact with a new friend or group
- making contact with a lost friend
- getting help from friends on the site
- social gaming on the site
- a decision to defriend someone
- a problem that happened while using the site

Quiz 1

a What do you remember about Unit 1? Answer all the questions you can and then check in the Student's Book.

1 Which sentence is true (✓) about the girl in picture A?

A She is writing a PhD paper. ☐
B She works for Microsoft. ☐
C She travelled round the USA two years ago. ☐

2 Match the two parts of the sentences.

1 I use my phone ☐
2 I first met Marco ☐
3 I'm doing some research ☐
4 I was shopping in town ☐

A in 2010.
B when you rang me.
C about ten times a day.
D at the moment.

3 Circle the correct words.

I don't know / I'm not knowing what Ali *does / was doing* yesterday. I *sent / was sending* him a text at 4 o'clock, but he *doesn't / didn't* answer it.

4 Match the words to make expressions for online communication.

1 digital — A network
2 privacy — B footprint
3 social — C settings

5 Complete the sentence.

A .... is a connection to another web page on the internet.

6 Choose the correct answer: A, B or C.

If you turn up your TV,
A it gets power from the electricity supply.
B the sound becomes louder.
C you can search for programmes that you want to watch.

7 Circle the correct words.

When you *make / set / come* up a new business, it usually takes time to *build / speed / charge* up public support for it.

8 Look at picture B. What is Sam Haber's hobby?

....

9 The verb forms are wrong in this sentence. Write the correct verbs.

When these performers [1]**have appeared** on YouTube in 2011, no one [2]**had been seeing** them before, but since then they [3]**became** very well known.

1 .... 2 ....
3 ....

10 Tick (✓) the words that contain the /tʃ/ sound.

catching ☐ action ☐
picture ☐ architect ☐

b 🔊9 Listen and check your answers.

c Now look at your Student's Book and write three more quiz questions for Unit 1.

Question: ....
....
Answer: ....

Question: ....
....
Answer: ....

Question: ....
....
Answer: ....

2 Well played!

1 Vocabulary

Sports equipment

a Write words 1–6 in the puzzle. Then use the ◯ letters to make one more word for sports equipment.

① ② ③ ④ ⑤ ⑥

1 ☐☐☐☐☐◯
2 ☐☐☐◯☐
3 ☐◯☐☐☐☐
4 ☐☐☐◯☐
5 ☐◯☐
6 ☐☐☐☐☐◯☐

☐☐☐☐☐☐

b Are the sentences *right* (✓) or *wrong* (✗)?

1 You can dive into a pool. ☐
2 A net is needed for a game of cricket. ☐
3 People do athletics on a court. ☐
4 You skate on an ice rink. ☐
5 Hockey players hit the ball with a racket. ☐
6 You wear pads to protect your eyes. ☐
7 A piste is used by people when they are skiing. ☐
8 Football matches are played on a football pitch. ☐

Help yourself!

Sports idioms

Match the idioms in **bold** with the meanings.

1 I thought I was doing well in Maths. It **took the wind out of my sails** when I only got 55% in the exam. ☐
2 You'll have to make a decision about this. **The ball is in your court**. ☐
3 He was **hitting below the belt** when he made a joke about my dad's illness. ☐
4 I **jumped the gun** when I told you that Julie and Luca were getting married. They actually haven't made a decision yet. ☐
5 I'll never be able to finish this job if you keep **moving the goal posts**. It's frustrating! ☐
6 I've spent ages on my Art project, but I'm **on the home straight** now. ☐
7 You're **skating on thin ice** with Louise. If she finds out you've been lying to her, she'll be extremely angry. ☐
8 I really didn't want to go to Gary's party. Your phone call **got me off the hook** – thanks! ☐

A in the last stages of a long project
B doing something unfair and cruel
C it's your responsibility to take action
D took away my positive and confident feelings
E taking a risk in a dangerous situation
F acted too soon
G gave me an escape from a difficult situation
H changing the rules or conditions for an activity without warning

Now match idioms 1–8 with the sports.

tennis	☐	ice skating	☐
fishing	☐	running (in a race)	☐
boxing	☐	sailing	☐
football	☐	horse racing	☐

2 Grammar Grammar reference: page 82

Infinitive and *-ing* review

Check it out!

Common verbs followed by *-ing*:

like love enjoy hate keep imagine recommend suggest avoid practise

Common verbs followed by infinitive:

begin decide want need plan choose prepare hope expect forget agree arrange offer promise pretend seem would like/love

a Circle the correct verb.

1 I enjoy *watching / to watch* the tennis on TV.
2 My brother is hoping *getting / to get* into the under-18 rugby team.
3 Does Sofia want *coming / to come* to the pool with us?
4 I'd love *buying / to buy* those skates, but they're too expensive.
5 Can you imagine *winning / to win* first prize in the lottery?
6 You'll need *bringing / to bring* your tennis racket with you tomorrow.
7 I don't recommend *using / to use* that sun cream. It isn't very good.
8 My computer keeps *crashing / to crash*. I don't know what to do about it.

b Complete the sentences. Use a preposition + *-ing* or *to* + infinitive.

1 We were lucky .... (get) tickets for the football match.
2 Amir is interested .... (join) the local tennis club.
3 I'm not very good .... (run).
4 It's very dangerous .... (ride) a motorbike without a helmet.
5 The dialogue was in French, but it was quite easy .... (understand).
6 I haven't made much progress .... (find) the information I need.
7 We're looking forward .... (see) you on Sunday.
8 The race was very exciting .... (watch).

c 10 Complete the dialogue with the correct form of the verbs. Then listen and check.

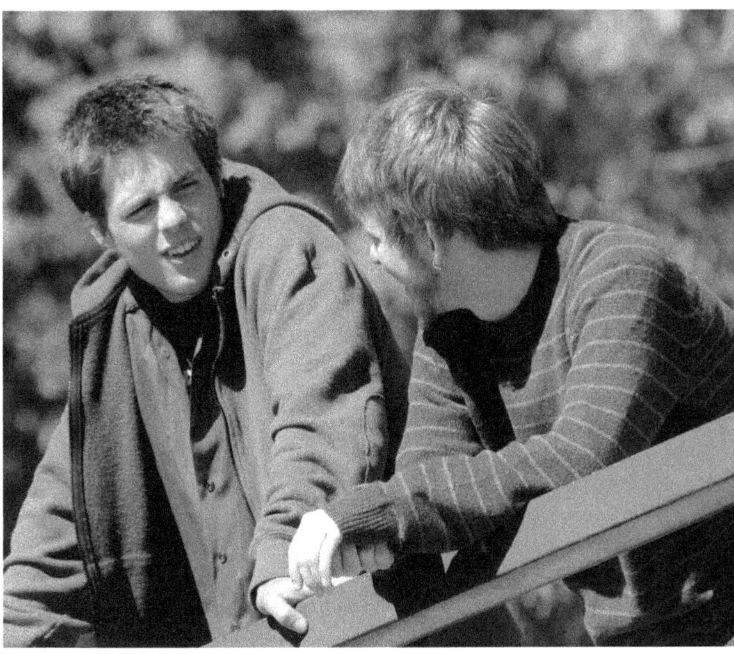

surf practise have come try skateboard go become learn start

Ben: Jamie and I have decided [1] .... skiing next month. How about [2] .... with us?

Karl: Oh, I don't know. I've never been skiing. I wouldn't know what to do.

Ben: Well, you love [3] .... – you spend all summer at the beach. And you're good at [4] .... I think you'd really enjoy skiing.

Karl: Yeah, I'd like [5] .... it. Is it difficult [6] ....?

Ben: Not really, but you'll need [7] .... some lessons. I recommend [8] .... in the beginners' class. The lessons aren't very expensive.

Karl: That sounds OK.

Ben: But don't expect [9] .... an expert overnight. You have to keep [10] .... so you develop your skills before you start skiing down a mountain.

3 Vocabulary

Sports collocations

Check it out!

Remember: the verbs *beat*, *win*, *break* and *hold* are irregular. See page 102.

a There is a mistake in each of these sentences. ~~Cross out~~ the wrong word and write the correct word.

1 Diana easily won all the other girls in the race.

....

2 The American athlete Bob Beamon broke the world record for the long jump for 23 years.

....

3 Cricket is a teams sport, with eleven players in each team.

....

4 Competition sports are exciting to watch because everyone is trying to win.

....

5 My team is staying at home this Saturday, so I'll probably go and watch the match.

....

6 Diving is an extreme sport – each person performs alone and the judges give points for each dive.

....

b Complete the sentences with sports collocations. Use words from both boxes.

break contact win score winter sports	sport sports points events the match the record

1 Lots of different .... are held here, including football, cricket and athletics.
2 In Australian Rules football, you .... six .... for a goal.
3 Because rugby is a .... , players are sometimes seriously injured.
4 Skiing and snowboarding are both ....
5 She's hoping to .... for the women's high jump in the next world championships.
6 This team is playing brilliantly. I'm sure they'll .... against France.

c Think of an example for each of the following.

1 a team that hasn't won a match lately

....

2 a player who often scores goals

....

3 a woman who holds a record in a sport

....

4 a place in your neighbourhood where sports events are held

....

5 a team sport that you have played

....

6 a sports event that is held every year

....

4 Listen

a 🔊 11 Listen to the quiz. Tick (✓) the correct sport for each question.

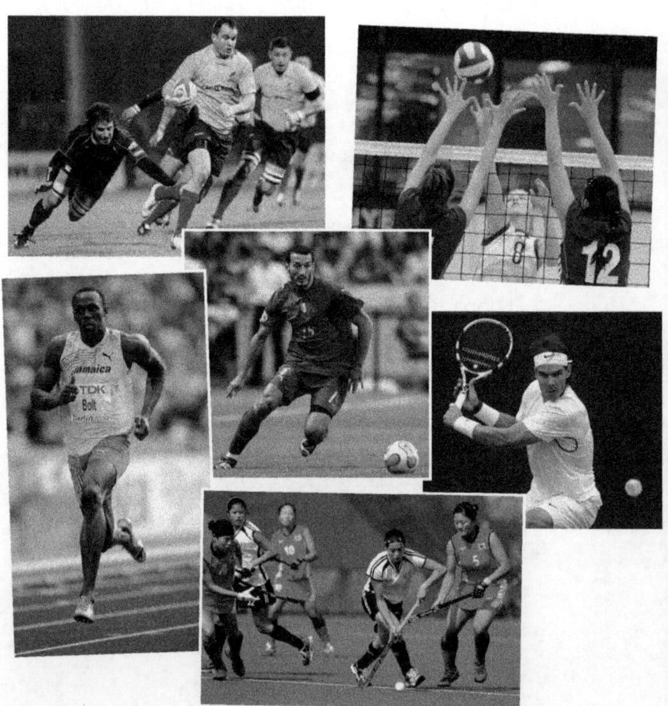

	1	2	3	4	5	6	7
Football							
Tennis							
Volleyball							
Hockey							
Running							
Rugby							

b 11 Listen again and answer the quiz questions. If you don't know an answer, make a guess or use the internet to find out.

1 ....
2 ....
3 ....
4 ....
5 ....
6 ....
7 ....

5 Grammar Grammar reference: page 82

remember, *stop* and *try* with *-ing* and the infinitive

a Read each sentence and then decide if the statement below is *right* (✓) or *wrong* (✗).

1 *I didn't remember to take out the rubbish.*
I forgot to take it out. ☐

2 *Debra is going to try using an exercise bike at the gym.*
She'll use an exercise bike if she can. ☐

3 *Dad stopped to get some eggs from the supermarket.*
He no longer buys eggs from the supermarket. ☐

4 *I don't remember meeting your cousin.*
I have no memory of this meeting. ☐

5 *We tried to contact Silvio this morning.*
We didn't succeed in contacting him. ☐

6 *I've stopped watching this programme.*
I stopped doing something else so I could watch this programme. ☐

b Complete the sentences with the correct form of the verbs.

1 The pizzas at this place aren't very good now. We've stopped .... (buy) them.
2 Why don't you try .... (skydive)? I think you'd enjoy it.
3 Please remember .... (post) this letter on your way home.
4 When we get to the top of the hill, I want to stop .... (have) a drink.
5 You must try .... (do) well in your final exams this year.
6 I remember .... (love) this song when I was younger.

6 Pronunciation

Homophones

a 12 (Circle) the two homophones. Then listen, check and repeat.

1	nose	noise	knows
2	soon	son	sun
3	eat	ate	eight
4	by	boy	buy
5	saw	sore	sure
6	weak	wake	week
7	were	wear	where
8	been	bean	bin

b 13 Complete the sentences with pairs of homophones. Then listen and repeat.

1 Yesterday I .... my bike along the .... beside the river.
2 Unfortunately, he .... the ball .... the window.
3 Alex and Jill are coming over and .... bringing .... skateboards with them.
4 I .... your watch was broken, so I bought you a .... one.
5 I can't .... any music, so I guess the band isn't playing .... tonight.

c 14 There are three mistakes with homophones in each sentence. Write the correct sentence. Then listen and repeat.

1 Wheel be ready buy half passed eight.
....
....
2 They aunt sure weather they'll be a loud to come.
....
....
3 No one nose wear Julie was last weak.
....
....

15 Practise saying these words

court goalkeeper individual league reduce referee skates specific spectacular spectator tournament whistle

7 Read

a Read the competition rules and Rosa's competition entry. Tick (✓) the photo that she describes.

Sports Photo Competition

WIN two tickets to a sports event of your choice plus free travel, meals and ★★★ hotel accommodation for 2 nights **plus** £500 spending money!

- Send in your favourite photo of a sports activity.
- Give some information about this sport and its rules.
- Describe the photo and explain why you have chosen it.

All entries must be received by 1st October.

A

B

C

Ice hockey is played on an ice rink with a goal net at each end. Two teams on skates compete to score goals by using a stick, curved at one end, to hit a small, hard rubber disc, called a puck. There may be 20 players in each team, but only six can be on the rink at any time. One of them is the goalkeeper, who is allowed to catch the puck or block it with any part of their body, as well as with their stick. Ice hockey has always been most popular in places with cold winters, for example Canada, northern European countries and the northern states of the USA. However, with indoor ice rinks, many other countries have started competing in this sport and ice hockey events are held all year round.

This photo was taken during a match between Hungary and Holland. Two players are trying to control the puck, which is bouncing up on the right. Their bodies are bumping together and the Dutch player is finding it hard to keep his balance on one leg, but they are both concentrating on reaching the puck with their sticks.

I chose this action photo because it shows how exciting and competitive the game is. The light shining on the ice gives you an idea of the hard surface, which makes ice hockey the fastest team sport in the world. The puck can travel up to 160 kph and players may skate at about 40 kph. They must be ready to race forward, stop or turn quickly and change suddenly from attacking to defending.

Also, as the photo shows, ice hockey is a very physical contact sport. Injuries are common, especially when players crash into each other. In the photo you can see the helmets that protect their heads and the thick pads that are worn on their legs, knees and shoulders. The game is so challenging that players can usually only stay on the ice for about two minutes before being replaced. It is their amazing physical skill and speed that make ice hockey so exciting to watch.

Rosa Franklin

b Choose the correct answer: A, B or C.

1 The winner of the competition
- **A** can choose to stay in any hotel.
- **B** will win a prize that includes cash.
- **C** will be chosen in September.

2 There are always … on the rink in an ice hockey match.
- **A** twenty players
- **B** six players
- **C** two goalkeepers

3 Ice hockey is
- **A** a winter sport.
- **B** a competitive sport.
- **C** an individual sport.

4 The players in the photo are
- **A** in European teams.
- **B** trying to hit the ball.
- **C** trying to score a goal.

5 Players are often injured in ice hockey because
- **A** it is a contact sport.
- **B** they don't use protective equipment.
- **C** they go faster than any other athletes.

6 Rosa really enjoys watching this sport because
- **A** the puck travels very fast.
- **B** the players crash into each other.
- **C** the players are fast and skilful.

Write an entry for the Sports Photo Competition. You can:

- use a photo that you have taken
- download a photo from the internet
- find a photo in a magazine or newspaper

Quiz 2

a What do you remember about Unit 2? Answer all the questions you can and then check in the Student's Book.

A

B

C

1 **In which country do men and women play the sport in picture A?** ....

2 **Circle the odd one out.**

clubs rackets goggles sticks

3 **Can you find four words for sports equipment in the puzzle in B? Each word contains the letter A.**

....

....

4 **Complete the sentence with the correct form of the verbs.**

I love [1] .... (run) and I expect [2] .... (do) quite well in the marathon, but I can't imagine [3] .... (win) it.

5 **How many times was the football World Cup held between 2000 and 2012?**

....

6 **Complete the sentence about the athlete in picture C.**

In 2009 he succeeded in .... the world .... for the 100 metres sprint.

7 **Circle the correct verbs.**

Argentina *beat / broke / won* Germany when they *held / played / scored* a goal in the last minute of the match.

8 **Match the expressions with the examples.**

1 sports kit	**A** football, rugby
2 individual sports	**B** net, board
3 contact sports	**C** golf, skiing
4 sports equipment	**D** shorts, boots

9 **Read this sentence and then decide if the statements below are *right* (✓) or *wrong* (✗).**

I don't remember taking my sunglasses to the picnic.

A I left my sunglasses at home. ☐

B I definitely didn't forget to take my sunglasses. ☐

C Maybe I took my sunglasses, but I can't remember. ☐

10 **Complete the sentence with a pair of homophones.**

We spent an .... finishing .... homework.

b 🔊 16 Listen and check your answers.

c Now look at your Student's Book and write three more quiz questions for Unit 2.

Question: ....
....
Answer: ....

Question: ....
....
Answer: ....

Question: ....
....
Answer: ....

3 Multicultural matters

1 Grammar Grammar reference: page 78

be used to and *get used to*

a Choose the correct answer: A, B or C.

1 It's a small flat so the boys will have to .... used to sharing a room.
  A get **B** be **C** getting
2 My sister was homesick at first, but now she's used .... in London.
  A live **B** to live **C** to living
3 I love Rome, but I still can't .... the noise of the traffic!
  A use to **B** be used to **C** get used to
4 Sorry, I can't finish my dessert. .... to eating a big meal at lunch time.
  A I'm not used **B** I don't use **C** I didn't use
5 I hated the rain when I first moved to England, but .... to it now.
  A I used **B** I'm used **C** I'm use
6 Matt found his new job confusing at first, but .... used to it now.
  A he **B** he's getting **C** he's being

b There is a mistake in each of these sentences. ~~Cross out~~ the wrong word and write the correct word.

1 Jill was anxious at first because she wasn't used to drive in the city.
....
2 Daniel used to sitting next to me when we were in primary school.
....
3 It's difficult to be used to the cold weather in the winter here.
....
4 I didn't used to like jazz music, but I enjoy it now.
....
5 Karen's late again! She doesn't used to getting up early in the morning.
....
6 My grandparents can't get use to living in a small flat without a garden.
....

Check it out!

Remember, we use *used to* + infinitive for things that happened in the past but don't happen now. Don't forget the negative and question forms.

*She's retired now, but she **used to work** in the local hospital.*

*He looks different. He **didn't use to have** such short hair.*

***Did** you **use to be** scared of the dark?*

2 Vocabulary

Extended family

a Circle the correct words.

1 **Grace:** Andy is my grandfather and his mother is Sara. She's my *grandmother / great-grandmother.*
2 **Lou:** My *cousins / nephews* are Josh and Owen. They're my sister's children.
3 **Elena:** I'm married to Owen's brother Josh. That means I'm Owen's *sister-in-law / half sister.*
4 **Alice:** I'm Josh's *wife / ex-wife*. We're divorced now.
5 **Sam:** Lou is my grandmother's brother, so he's my *father-in-law / great-uncle.*
6 **Andy:** My wife's mum is Emma, so she's my *stepmother / mother-in-law.*

b Use the information in Exercise 2a to complete the family tree.

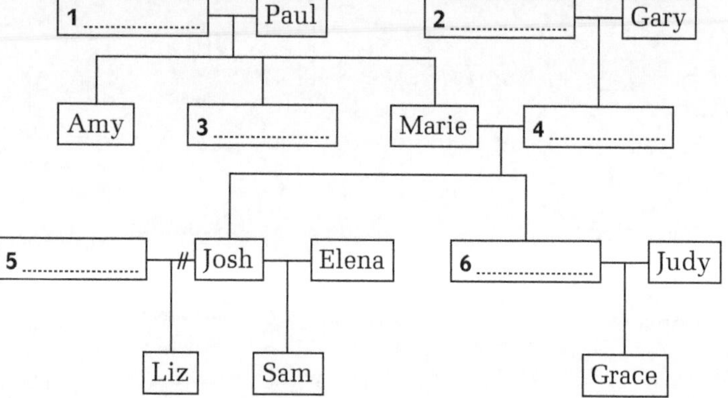

c 17 Look at the family tree in Exercise 2b and complete the sentences. Then listen and check.

1 .... is Josh's second wife.
2 .... is Liz's stepbrother.
3 .... is Grace's great-aunt.
4 Andy is Judy's ....
5 Lou is Andy's ....
6 Liz and Grace are Gary's ....

3 Read

a Read the text. Which person found it easiest to make the change to a new country?

....

In 2007–2009 three generations of the Thompson family moved from the UK to start a new life in Italy. Here they describe their experiences of adapting to a new environment.

Diane

I met my second husband, Francesco, when he was on holiday in the UK, and when we got married in 2007 I moved to Italy with my daughter Ruth. For the first year we lived with Francesco's parents in Parma, and this was a difficult time. His family is very close and I used to feel like an outsider in the house, especially with his mother. Although I'd learnt some Italian, I couldn't speak it well enough to express what I really wanted to say and it was very frustrating. Things gradually got easier when we moved into our own home. I've now got a much better relationship with Francesco's family and I'm more confident with the language. I still miss my father and my English friends, but we keep in touch through the internet and I go back for visits quite often.

Ruth

I didn't want to move away from the UK because it meant leaving all my friends behind. I'd always loved going to Italy on holiday, but actually living in a foreign country is very different from being a tourist. When I first started school in Parma I was totally confused! But I had a special teacher to help me with the language, which I picked up quickly, and now it's more natural for me to speak Italian than English. Also I soon got to know a great group of kids at school, who have become my best friends. So I've adapted well to the life here and can't imagine being anywhere else. If I had to move back to England now, I'd feel like a foreigner!

Don

I'd been living alone since my wife died, and a year after Diane and Francesco set up their new home they persuaded me to come and join them. There's plenty of room in their house and I get on well with Francesco and all his family. And Parma is a lovely city, with the most wonderful food! But I just couldn't get used to living there. It was partly because of the heat in summer, and because the countryside is flat and I'm not used to that. But also I didn't like losing my independence. I used to miss little things, like going down to the local shops and chatting with friends I'd known all my life. In the end I decided to come back home. It was too hard for me to put down new roots in another country, and I'm happier where I am.

b Complete the sentences with the correct names.

1 .... has a good relationship with his/her son-in-law.
2 .... used to have a lot of problems communicating with people.
3 .... made new friends easily in Italy.
4 .... didn't use to get on very well with his/her mother-in-law.
5 .... couldn't get used to the weather in Parma.
6 .... soon got used to speaking a foreign language.
7 .... is used to living in a place where there are hills.
8 .... would find it hard to get used to living in the UK now.
9 .... became happier with his/her life in 2008.

4 Vocabulary

British/American vocabulary

a Write the American English words for 1–9 in the puzzle. Then use the ◯ letters to make one more American English expression.

1 HOLIDAY ☐☐☐☐☐◯☐☐
2 RUBBISH ☐☐☐☐☐☐◯
3 LORRY ☐◯☐☐☐
4 AUTUMN ◯☐☐☐
5 PETROL ☐☐◯
6 GARDEN ☐☐◯☐
7 BISCUIT ☐☐☐☐☐◯
8 TROUSERS ☐☐◯☐☐
9 SWEETS ◯☐☐☐☐

☐☐☐☐☐ H   F ☐☐☐☐

b Write the words for the definitions. Use the words from Exercise 4a.

Definition	British	American
1 clothing that covers your legs	....	....
2 a place where you can grow plants	....	....
3 potato pieces cooked in oil	....	....
4 a large type of road vehicle	....	....
5 liquid which provides energy for cars	....	....
6 a small hard cake that you eat as a snack	....	....
7 the season after summer	....	....
8 unwanted things that you throw away	....	....
9 small sweet snacks containing sugar	....	....
10 a time when you go away from home to relax	....	....

Help yourself!

British and American spelling

There are some differences in spelling between British and American English. Look at these examples:

British	American
colour	*color*
realise	*realize*
centre	*center*
traveller	*traveler*

Underline the words with the American spelling and write the British spelling. Use a dictionary to help.

1 We often socialize with our neighbors.
....

2 They traveled for 2 hours before they realized they were lost.
....

3 Our teacher is organizing a trip to the theater.
....

4 I've memorized the words of my favorite songs.
....

5 Are you going to apologize for your behavior?
....

5 Pronunciation

British and American pronunciation

a 18 Listen to these words. Which type of pronunciation do you hear first and which second? Write 1 and 2.

Listen to the letter *r*.

	UK	US
a door	☐	☐
b turn	☐	☐
c sister	☐	☐
d search	☐	☐

Listen to the vowels.

	UK	US
e class	☐	☐
f watch	☐	☐
g tomato	☐	☐
h stupid	☐	☐

b 19 Listen and underline the stressed syllable. You will hear the British speaker first and then the American speaker.

	UK	US
1	weekend	weekend
2	magazine	magazine
3	laboratory	laboratory
4	advertisement	advertisement
5	kilometre	kilometer
6	address	address

c 20 Listen and write *UK* or *US*.

1. a warm bath ....
2. a bottle of water ....
3. a class of twenty students ....
4. forty kilometres/kilometers an hour ....
5. serve it with tomato sauce ....
6. a library in New York ....

d 21 Listen to a British speaker and then an American speaker saying the phrases in Exercise 5c. Then listen again and repeat.

22 Practise saying these words

accent acceptance brother-in-law
bully fluently gradually marriage
neighbourhood picturesque recognise
unnecessary value

6 Grammar Grammar reference: page 82

as, *like* and *such as*

a Read each sentence and then decide if the statement below is *right* (✓) or *wrong* (✗).

1. *I often eat Japanese food, such as sushi and yakitori.*
   Sushi and yakitori are examples of Japanese food. ☐
2. *Luke works as a laboratory assistant in the Science Institute.*
   Luke's job is similar to a lab assistant's job. ☐
3. *We can use sunlight as a way of producing energy.*
   Sunlight can be used for this purpose. ☐
4. *I'd love to be able to play the guitar like Eduardo.*
   Eduardo and I would like to be good guitarists. ☐
5. *Eva is keen to travel through South America by train, as her sister did.*
   Eva wants to travel in the same way as her sister. ☐
6. *My brother doesn't look like me.*
   My brother's personality isn't similar to mine. ☐

b Tick (✓) the sentence if it is correct. If there is a mistake, ~~cross it out~~ and write the correct word(s).

1. Big cities like London and New York are home to people of many nationalities.
   ....
2. Hungarian is generally regarded like a difficult language to learn.
   ....
3. I don't speak English fluently such as Paula does.
   ....
4. James got top marks in Spanish, just as you predicted.
   ....
5. What does your new language class like? Are you enjoying it?
   ....
6. French is an official language in many African countries, as Senegal and Guinea.
   ....

c Use the table to make seven sentences.

Josef is good at competitive sports		a journalist.
I don't often eat red meat, such		German.
My great-aunt used to work in Spain	as	professional singers.
New York is often referred to	like	beef and lamb.
The Dutch language is a bit		'the Big Apple'.
He's hoping to study at Cambridge University,		rugby and basketball.
Their music is amazing – they sound		his parents did.

1 ....
2 ....
3 ....
4 ....
5 ....
6 ....
7 ....

7 Listen

a 23 Listen to the interview about multiculturalism in the city of Liverpool. Tick (✓) the topics that are discussed.

music ☐ food ☐ shops ☐ clothes ☐
festivals ☐ languages ☐ historical information ☐

b Choose the correct answer: A, B or C.

1 The largest immigrant communities in Liverpool are from
  - **A** China, Africa and India.
  - **B** Africa and South America.
  - **C** Asia and South America.

2 .... per cent of people in Liverpool are from non-British backgrounds.
  - **A** Four
  - **B** Fourteen
  - **C** Over forty

LIVERPOOL

3 Liverpool used to be
  - **A** a multicultural city.
  - **B** more popular with migrants than London.
  - **C** the second most important city in the UK.

4 People didn't come to Liverpool to live in the 1980s because
  - **A** it wasn't big enough.
  - **B** it was very difficult to find a job.
  - **C** there were a lot of immigrants.

5 Africa Oyé, the International Street Festival and Brazilica are
  - **A** festivals which took place in July.
  - **B** events which are held every year.
  - **C** the only multicultural events in Liverpool.

6 Liverpool has
  - **A** a great variety of restaurants.
  - **B** more restaurants than other British cities.
  - **C** more interesting food than other parts of the UK.

Write an article for a school magazine or website on multicultural life in your area. Think about four or more of the topics in Exercise 7a and do some research to check that your information is correct.

Quiz 3

a What do you remember about Unit 3? Answer all the questions you can and then check in the Student's Book.

A
B
Let's stop for a burger and fries at the gas station.

1 Look at picture A. Where was this boy born?

....

2 Match the sentences.

1 I'm getting used to this job.
2 I used to work in this job.
3 I'm used to this job.

A I don't work in this job now.
B The job seems normal now.
C The job is becoming less strange.

3 Circle the correct words.

Angela used to [1] *live / living* in Hamburg so she [2] *used / was used* to speaking German. Now she's moved to Lisbon and has to [3] *be / get* used to a new language.

4 Which foreign language is studied most often by secondary students in the UK?

....

5 Complete the table.

Male	Female
brother-in-law	1 ....
2	great-aunt
ex-husband	3 ....
4	mother-in-law

6 Complete the sentence with words for family members.

My mother and father got divorced in 2009. Mum's second husband Philip is my .... and their daughter is my ....

7 Circle the odd one out.

autumn vacation lorry rubbish

8 Look at picture B. Are these people in the UK or the USA?

....

9 Write the American words.

A garden ....
B trousers ....
C biscuit ....

10 Complete the sentences with *as* or *like*.

This looks [1] .... a nice restaurant. I'd like to get a job [2] .... a waitress in a place [3] .... this.

b 24 Listen and check your answers.

c Now look at your Student's Book and write three more quiz questions for Unit 3.

Question: ....
....
Answer: ....

Question: ....
....
Answer: ....

Question: ....
....
Answer: ....

4 Adrenaline rush

1 Vocabulary

Verbs of fear

a Put the boxes in order and write the words in the correct list.

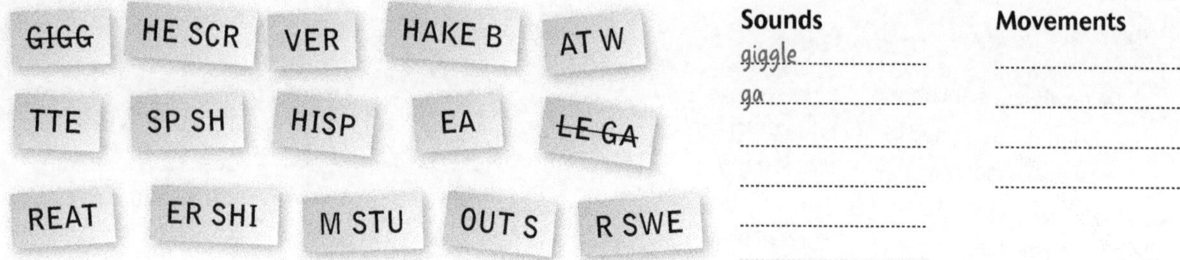

Sounds	Movements
giggle	....
ga........................	....
....	....
....	....
....	
....	

b Complete the sentences. Use verbs from Exercise 1a in the correct form.

1 She's .... because she's cold.
2 His hands are ....
3 She's .... in his ear.
4 She can .... under water.
5 He's .... because it's hot.
6 The girls are ....

Help yourself!

Sound and meaning

Verbs like *stutter*, *giggle* and *gasp* imitate the sounds they describe.

Try to guess what these verbs mean from their sound. Complete the sentences, using the verbs in the correct form. Then check in your dictionary.

knock growl rattle buzz gurgle smash

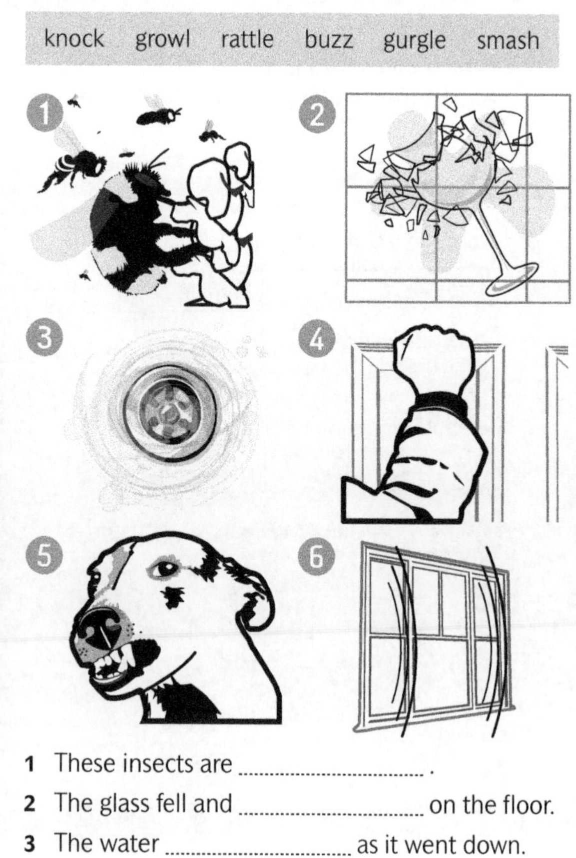

1 These insects are ....
2 The glass fell and .... on the floor.
3 The water .... as it went down.
4 Someone is .... on the door.
5 Dogs make me nervous when they ....
6 The windows were .... in the wind.

2 Grammar Grammar reference: page 84

Adverbs

a Complete the sentences with the adverbs. Then underline the word(s) that each adverb describes.

1 We walked ....slowly.......... (slow) through the park.
2 He put the glasses .... (careful) into the dishwasher.
3 I made some .... (incredible) stupid mistakes in the exam.
4 It was raining .... (heavy) during the night.
5 She speaks three languages .... (fluent).
6 I'm afraid the train is going to arrive .... (late).
7 These cakes taste .... (absolute) delicious.
8 His heart was beating .... (extreme) fast.

Check it out!

Check these spelling rules for forming adverbs from adjectives.

- Most adjectives: add *-ly*
  real → *real**ly*** *definite* → *definite**ly***
- Adjectives ending in *-y*: ~~y~~ + *-ily*
  happy → *happ**ily*** *busy* → *bus**ily***
- Adjectives ending in *-able* or *-ible*: ~~e~~ + *-y*
  comfortable → *comfortab**ly*** *terrible* → *terrib**ly***
- Adjectives ending in *-ic*: add *-ally*
  basic → *basic**ally*** *automatic* → *automatic**ally***
  Exception: *public* → *public**ly***

b 25 Complete the dialogue. Use adverbs from the adjectives in the box. Then listen and check.

loud safe fast good sudden personal absolute slow

A: What's the scariest thing you've ever done?
B: Doing a bungee jump. When I jumped off the tower I was [1] .... terrified and my friends told me I was screaming [2] .... all the way down.
A: So what does it feel like when you're falling?
B: Well, the ground seems to rush towards you incredibly [3] .... , and then [4] .... the rope pulls you up and it feels fantastic!
A: And after that, how do you land?
B: Oh, there's no problem with that. When you stop bouncing up and down, they just bring you [5] .... to the ground and there's someone there to make sure you land [6] .... in the right position. Still, at first I couldn't walk very [7] .... after I'd landed – my legs were like rubber!
A: Hmm. [8] .... , I don't think I'd enjoy doing that.

3 Pronunciation

Stressing adverbs and adjectives

a 26 Listen and practise saying the pairs of sentences.

1 It was quite good.
It was really fantastic.
2 You look very nice.
You look absolutely gorgeous!
3 He felt a bit sad.
He felt incredibly unhappy.
4 They're very tired.
They're completely exhausted.

b 27 Underline the words that have extra stress to show strong feeling. Then listen and repeat.

1 It was so exciting!
2 It was just brilliant!
3 That rollercoaster is really amazing!
4 Honestly, it was the worst film I've ever seen!
5 I've never heard such a stupid comment!

28 Practise saying these words

breath breathe chemical completely emotional investigator liquid scary scream shiver sweat whisper

4 Read

a Read the text and choose the correct answer: A, B or C.

A *daredevil* is a person who

A has amazing skills as an acrobat.

B enjoys doing unusually dangerous things.

C performs publicly for a large audience.

The daredevils of Niagara

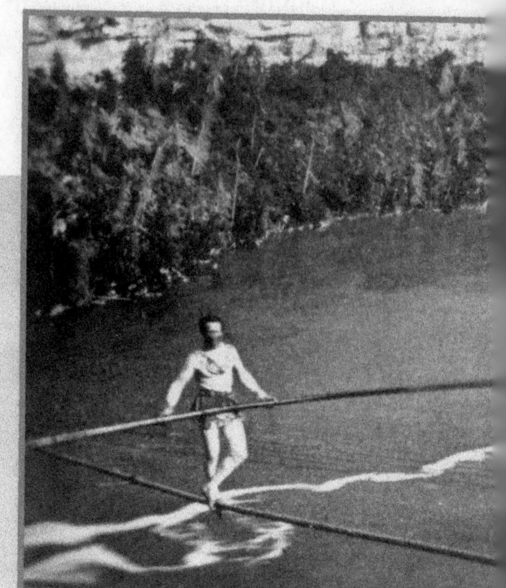

Niagara Falls, on a river that flows between Canada and the USA, are world famous. The largest of three waterfalls here has a drop of 53 metres – the height of an 18-storey building – and over two million litres of water per second plunge down into the gorge below. It is a [1] .... dramatic sight. It is also famous for the many daredevils who have risked their lives here.

In 1859 Jean François Gravelet, known as 'the Great Blondin', stretched a rope 335 metres long over the gorge and walked across it, to the amazement of the crowd who came to watch. Within two years, Blondin had repeated this performance over 20 times, adding more and more [2] .... stunts. He lay on the rope, stood on his head and walked backwards. Sometimes he crossed with his eyes covered, or with his feet and hands tied. Once, he balanced a table on the rope and sat down to drink champagne. On another day he brought a stove and cooked omelettes to send down to the passengers in a boat below. Three times he carried another man on his back – his most difficult and dangerous stunt.

People later copied Blondin's performances. Others swam across the terrifying waters below the waterfall, sailed through them in boats or jumped in from great heights. But the first person to go over the waterfall itself was an [3] .... unusual daredevil. In 1901, on her 63rd birthday, ex-schoolteacher Annie Taylor climbed into a wooden barrel which floated out into the river above the waterfall. Then [4] .... it disappeared in the torrent of water going over the falls. Nobody expected Annie to survive, but 30 minutes later a rescue boat found the barrel and she stepped out, unhurt except for a cut on her head.

Others since then have not been so [5] .... Of the 15 people who have gone over the falls in a barrel or other device, five died. The last person to challenge Niagara was Kirk Jones, who went down in 2003 with no protection at all, not even a barrel. Incredibly, he survived. But times have changed since the days of Blondin and Taylor. Instead of a crowd of [6] .... spectators, the police were waiting when Jones came out of the water, and he was fined $4,400 for doing an [7] .... stunt.

b Complete the text with the adjectives and adverbs in the box.

excited	amazing	illegal	lucky	suddenly	spectacularly	extremely

c Are the sentences *right* (✓) or *wrong* (✗)?

1 Lots of people came to see Blondin's first walk across the gorge at Niagara. ☐
2 Blondin did exactly the same acrobatic tricks on the rope more than 20 times. ☐
3 Another man walked across the rope three times with Blondin. ☐
4 Annie Taylor's stunt was especially unusual because she was a middle-aged woman. ☐
5 Annie was seriously injured when she was inside the barrel. ☐
6 Fifteen people have survived after going down the waterfall. ☐
7 Kirk Jones was the last person to ride down the waterfall in a barrel. ☐
8 Kirk had to pay a lot of money because he had broken the law. ☐

5 Vocabulary

Expressions of fear

a Match the two parts of the sentences.

1 My heart missed	☐	**A**	of my seat.
2 I had butterflies	☐	**B**	out of me.
3 I was on the edge	☐	**C**	a beat.
4 I nearly jumped out	☐	**D**	like a leaf.
5 It frightened the life	☐	**E**	in my stomach.
6 I was shaking	☐	**F**	of my skin.

b There is a mistake in each of these sentences. ~~Cross out~~ the wrong word and write the correct word.

1 The dreadful news made her heart run cold.

....

2 He was holding his breathe as he searched the list for his exam results.

....

3 When she suddenly saw the crocodile in the water, she almost jumped out from her skin.

....

4 His heart made a beat when she told him she was leaving.

....

5 Tell me what happened next! I'm on the back of my seat.

....

6 She had butterflies in the stomach as she waited to go on stage.

....

7 After the car accident, he was shivering like a leaf.

....

8 A huge spider suddenly ran across the wall. It frightened my life out of me!

....

6 Grammar Grammar reference: page 84

Making comparisons

Check it out!

Rules for forming comparative adverbs:

- If the adverb ends in *-ly*, the comparative is *more* + adverb.

Adjective	Adverb	Comparative adverb
slow	*slowly*	*more slowly*
happy	*happily*	*more happily*

- If the adverb has the same form as the adjective, the comparative is adverb + *-(e)r*.

hard	*hard*	*harder*
early	*early*	*earlier*

a Read each sentence and then decide if the statement below is *right* (✓) or *wrong* (✗).

1 *It rained more and more heavily as the day went on.*
The rain was extremely heavy all day. ☐

2 *The film isn't as funny as the book.*
The book is funnier than the film. ☐

3 *My old camera worked far more effectively than this one.*
This camera is a little worse than my old one. ☐

4 *The more powerful the speakers are, the better the sound will be.*
The sound depends on the quality of the speakers. ☐

b Put the words in order and write the sentences.

1 intelligent / fish / are / more / Dolphins / much / than

....

....

2 more / are / and / Computers / powerful / becoming / more

....

....

3 as / Cars / as / in the city / on motorways / quickly / can't travel

....

....

4 the more / went / we screamed / The faster / loudly / the roller coaster

....

....

5 fluently / a / me / than / Spanish / little / He / more / speaks

....

....

c Circle the correct words.

1 A: This bookshop is so expensive!
B: Yes, I agree. You can buy these books *more / more and more* cheaply on the internet.

2 A: Was your exam OK?
B: Yes, it was *much / more* easier than I expected.

3 A: What was the film like?
B: Well, it started slowly, but it got *more and more / as* exciting as it went on.

4 A: Is Danny's scooter better than yours?
B: There isn't much difference. Maybe it's *slightly / a great deal* faster than mine.

5 A: I didn't think football training would be *as / more* hard as this!
B: Yes, but the harder you practise, *the / so* more quickly you'll improve.

d Use your own ideas to complete the sentences.

1 .... are far more expensive than ....
2 You can travel a lot .... on a train than in a bus.
3 In my opinion, ... looks slightly .... than ....
4 I don't think .... sings as .... as ....
5 Recently I've been feeling more and more .... about ....

7 Listen

a 29 Listen to three people talking about old horror films. Which film is the oldest?

Psycho ☐ *Alien* ☐ *Night of the Lepus* ☐

b 29 Listen again and complete each sentence with two words.

1 *Psycho* doesn't have any modern ....
2 Marta thinks that some scenes from *Psycho* will .... the .... out of you.
3 She says that *Psycho* is an .... psychological thriller.
4 Ripley is the .... in *Alien*.
5 Patrick says that the monster in *Alien* is a .... creature.
6 He thinks the second film in the series was almost .... as *Alien*.
7 The monsters in *Night of the Lepus* are ....
8 The film-makers wanted it to be a serious ....
9 However, Alison and her friends giggled during the film because they thought the whole idea was ....

Write a review of a horror film or a scary episode in a TV series that you have seen recently. Include:

- some facts about the film/programme (date, director, actors, setting …)
- a brief account of the story (but don't spoil the ending!)
- your opinions

Quiz 4

a What do you remember about Unit 4? Answer all the questions you can and then check in the Student's Book.

(A)

(B)

1 **Look at picture A and complete the sentence.**

They're riding on a .... and they're ....ing.

2 **Which two letters do you need to make these three verbs of fear?**

_ w _ a t   _ h a k _   _ h i v _ r

3 **Match the verbs with the definitions.**

1 stutter ☐
2 gasp ☐
3 whisper ☐

A to take a sudden breath with your mouth open
B to speak very quietly
C to have difficulty saying words clearly

4 **Write the adverb forms.**

happy ....
incredible ....
hard ....

5 **Rewrite the sentence, adding the adverb form of the adjectives.**

I think the film is too long, although it's powerful. (personal, extreme)

....

....

6 **Circle the correct words.**

When she saw the letter her heart missed a *beat* / *breath*, and she had butterflies in her *heart* / *stomach* as she started to open it.

7 **Make three sentences.**

A You frightened the life out **B** I nearly jumped out **C** I was on the edge	of	my skin. my seat. me.

8 **Look at picture B. What film is this and when was it made?**

....

9 **Tick the correct sentence(s).**

You got 90% in the exam, but I only got 58%.

A My mark is slightly lower than yours. ☐
B You did much better in the exam than me. ☐
C You got a far higher mark than me. ☐
D Your mark is a bit higher than mine. ☐

10 **Circle the correct words.**

A: A phone isn't as good *as* / *than* a camera for taking photos.
B: No, but you can take photos more *easy* / *easily* with a phone.

b 30 Listen and check your answers.

c Now look at your Student's Book and write three more quiz questions for Unit 4.

Question: ....
....
Answer: ....

Question: ....
....
Answer: ....

Question: ....
....
Answer: ....

5 Man and beast

1 Vocabulary

The animal kingdom

a Circle the correct words.

1 Cats *are / aren't* rare animals.
2 I think it's cruel to keep birds in a *cage / sanctuary*.
3 A tame animal *is / isn't* used to humans.
4 Some animals are *hunted / endangered* for their fur.
5 Animals need food and water for their *species / survival*.
6 They took the injured lion to an animal *habitat / sanctuary*.

b Read the sentences and complete the crossword.

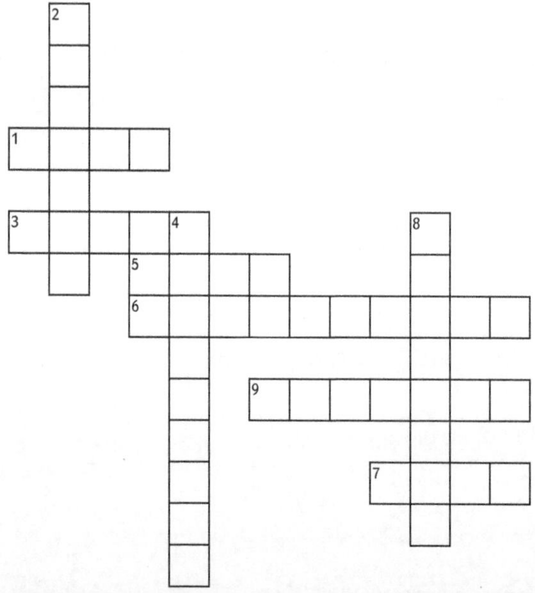

A The [1]........ animals in this safari park can move around freely in their natural [2]........ . They aren't kept in [3]........ .

B Josef works at a [4]........ for animals that have been hurt or badly treated. The elephant in this photo was brought here because it was injured. It has become very [5]........ and eats from Josef's hand.

C There used to be thousands of tigers in Asia, but now they're an [6]........ species, so they're very [7]........ . Their [8]........ depends on efforts to protect their environment and to stop people from [9]........ them.

Help yourself!

Animal idioms

Try to guess these idioms. Complete the sentences with the names of the animals in the box. Then match the idioms with the definitions (A–E).

cat	wolf	bull	sheep	rat

1 She's the **black** .... of her family. The others are all doctors. ☐
2 He's a **lone** .... He doesn't hang out with other people. ☐
3 The **fat** ....**s** who own the companies get huge salaries. ☐
4 You have to **take the** .... **by the horns** and deal with the problem! ☐
5 Something's not right here! I **smell a** .... ☐

A to suspect that something is wrong or someone is dishonest
B someone who doesn't work hard but gets lots of money
C a family member who is very different from the others
D to face a problem directly and take action
E a person who prefers to live and act alone

A

C

2 Grammar Grammar reference: page 86

Expressing contrast

a Match the two parts of the sentences.

1 He hasn't got any pets, even ☐
2 His computer still isn't working in spite ☐
3 You occasionally see wolves here, ☐
4 People sometimes camp here despite the fact ☐
5 David was shivering, although ☐
6 He climbed to the top of the tower despite ☐

A it wasn't cold.
B that it is illegal.
C his fear of heights.
D though he loves animals.
E of his attempts to repair it.
F though they're very rare.

b Complete the sentences so that the meaning is the same. Use the word(s) in brackets.

1 An elephant may weigh over 5,000 kg, but it is able to run quite fast.
(although)
An elephant can ....
....

2 Gorillas are an endangered species. However, they are still hunted.
(even)
....
...., they are still hunted.

3 It was raining, but we enjoyed our visit to the animal sanctuary.
(the rain)
We enjoyed our visit to the animal sanctuary
....

4 Sharks don't often attack humans, but almost everyone is scared of them.
(the fact)
Almost everyone is scared of sharks, ...
....
....

5 Penguins swim under water. However, they can't breathe like fish.
(though)
Penguins can't ....
....

c Complete the sentences using your own ideas.

1 Although ....
.... ,
we had a good time.
2 ...., in spite of the weather.
3 Many people say ....
...., though I don't agree.

3 Listen

a 31 Listen to the conversation about a news article. What is the article about? Choose the correct answer: A, B or C.

A The survival of wolves in the wild
B The danger of wolves becoming extinct
C Bringing wolves back to the UK

b 31 Listen again and answer the questions.

1 When did wolves become extinct in the UK?
....
2 Two places are mentioned where wolves still live in the wild. What are they?
....
3 How many wolves would be needed for the species to survive?
....
4 According to some people, why would wolves help to bring money into the country?
....
5 Which animals have a population that is too large?
....
6 According to farmers, which animals would be in danger from wolves?
....

c What do you think about the ideas in the article? Prepare to talk about this in your next lesson.

4 Vocabulary

Physical habits

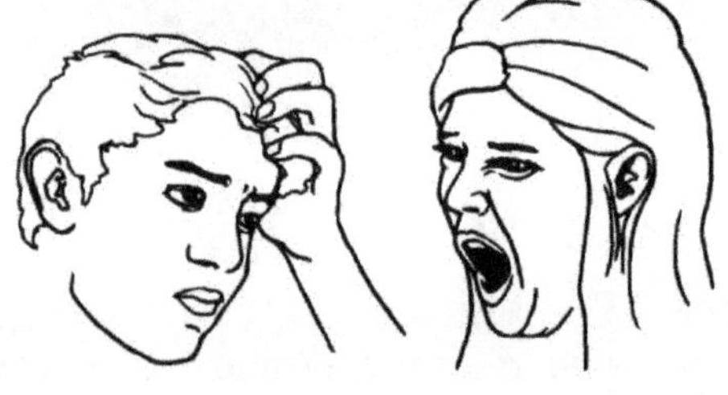

a Make eight verbs for physical habits. Use one letter from each column.

1 Y	A	W	N	■	2				
3				■	4				■
■	■	5						■	■
■	6							■	■
7						■	8		

		C	N		B		P		
	S	E	E		C	U	R		
S	N	W	I	A	T	L	R	P	
Y	H	E	W	Z	B	C	H	N	B
C	A	H	R	C	E	U	I	U	K

b Write the verbs from Exercise 4a in the correct list.

Using your mouth	....
Using your nose	....
Using your fingers	....
Using your eyes	....

c Complete the sentences. Use verbs from Exercise 4b in the correct form.

1 Everyone coughs and .... when they've got a cold.

2 Why are you .... your eyes? Are they sore?

3 I was so tired! I kept .... all the way through the film.

4 I must have .... as you took the photo. My eyes are closed.

5 Don't .... that mosquito bite. Use this cream instead.

6 A: I can't stop ....

B: Try holding your breath. That often helps.

5 Pronunciation

Pronunciation of *ea*

a 32 Look at the letters *ea* in these word pairs and decide if the vowel sound is the same (*S*) or different (*D*). Then listen, check and repeat.

1	mean	meat	☐
2	fear	wear	☐
3	speak	steak	☐
4	heavy	healthy	☐
5	realise	theatre	☐
6	great	repeat	☐
7	dear	dead	☐
8	season	reason	☐
9	nearly	early	☐
10	break	breakfast	☐

b 33 Find two ways through the puzzle. Follow the words which contain the /e/ sounds and /iː/ sounds. Then listen, check and repeat.

Start /e/ ↓ **Finish** /iː/ ↑

dead	ready	fear	cereal	repeat
hear	weather	bread	heart	season
ideal	great	healthy	increase	easily
break	speak	head teacher	breathe	idea
real	cheap	breath	leather	wear
beach	meat	heard	heavy	measure

/iː/ ↑ **Start** /e/ ↓ **Finish**

c 34 Listen and practise saying these sentences.

These seats are really heavy!
They're cheap earrings, but they look great.
I nearly always eat cereal for breakfast.
We didn't realise what the teacher meant.
They've already tried to break into the theatre.

35 Practise saying these words

although cruel endangered
extinction observe rare sanctuary
scratch survival tragedy wolf yawn

6 Grammar Grammar reference: page 86

Reflexive pronouns and *each other*

a Complete the table.

Subject pronouns	Object pronouns	Reflexive pronouns
I	me	1 ....
you	2	yourself
he	3	4 ....
5	her	herself
it	it	6 ....
we	7	ourselves
you (plural)	you	8 ....
9	them	10 ....

b Circle the correct words.

1 He's hurt *him / himself.*

2 See you soon. Enjoy *yourself / yourselves*!

3 They really like *themselves / each other.*

4 We gave *ourselves / each other* the same present.

5 They're looking at *themselves / each other.*

c 36 Complete the dialogues with reflexive pronouns or *each other*. Then listen and check.

A: What's Matt doing over there by 1 ....? He seems a bit depressed.
B: He's had an argument with Carla, and now they aren't speaking to 2 ....
A: Carla gets angry too easily, I think. She should try to control 3 ....
B: It's Matt's fault too. Honestly, the two of them were shouting at 4 .... for about ten minutes.

A: You look pleased with 5 ....
B: Yes! I've just met this really nice girl. She's one of Tara's friends.
A: Oh yeah? What's her name?
B: Well, she introduced 6 .... as Alexandra, but everyone calls her Allie. She and Tara have known 7 .... for ages. Anyway, she's given me her phone number and we're going to see 8 .... again next week.

7 Read

a Read the information page about bats and find the correct place (1–4) for the headings. There is one extra heading.

A Are special conditions necessary in the home?
B Do I need experience with bats to become a carer?
C How do I feed a bat?
D Are bats dangerous?
E Why does a bat need help?

About bats

People are often fearful of bats. But despite their association with scary castles and vampires in horror films, bats are intelligent, sensitive and sociable animals. Although they can't see well in the dark, their amazing 'echolocation' system allows them to find their way around by bouncing sound off the objects around them. They normally eat insects and fruit – this means they have an important role in reducing the insect population, and they help to spread the growth of forests. Although over 1,200 species of bat exist throughout the world, their numbers are falling, mainly because of damage to their habitat. In many countries they are protected by law but their survival is not certain.

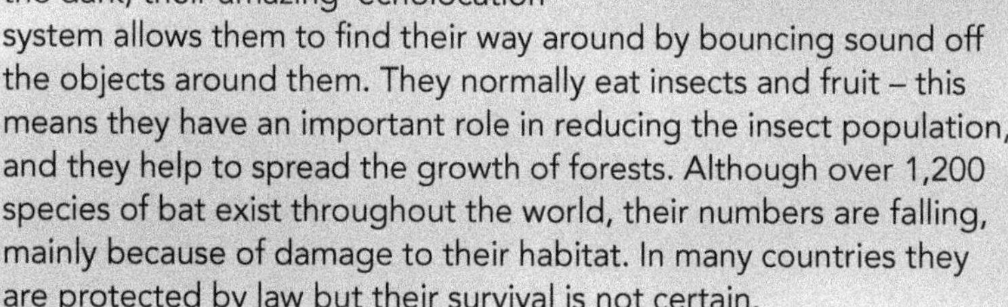

About us

We are a network of volunteers in the northwest region who rescue and care for bats that need help. People contact our centre when they find bats in trouble, and we organise carers to feed and look after the animals in their homes until they can be released back into the wild.

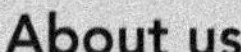

Becoming a bat carer: FAQs

1.....................
It may be a baby that has lost its mother and can't feed itself, or an older animal which is ill or injured. Bats are usually suffering from cold, thirst and stress when they come into our hands. They need specialised handling and feeding.

2.....................
No – we'll train you. And we'll put you in contact with other carers so that you can support each other and exchange information.

3.....................
No – but if they are frightened, they will try to defend themselves and may scratch or bite you. It's best to put on gloves when handling them.

4.....................
You will need an area that's quiet, warm and not too light, but you won't need a lot of space. Many of our carers use a bird cage for the bat to live in. You will also need a supply of special milk for babies and insects for adults. Our training sessions will help you with advice about feeding.

If you are interested in joining BatCare, please email us at **batcare@speedmail.org.uk.**

b Choose the correct answer: A, B or C.

1 Bats make people nervous
  A although they are sensitive and intelligent.
  B in spite of their appearance in horror films.
  C because they eat insects.

2 Bats can move around skilfully at night
  A because of their 'echolocation' system.
  B despite the fact that they are blind.
  C although they sometimes bump into objects.

3 The volunteers at BatCare
  A look after the bats at the BatCare centre.
  B keep the bats as pets.
  C help each other.

4 Bat carers shouldn't
  A pick up a bat if it is frightened.
  B hold a bat without wearing gloves.
  C worry if a bat scratches them.

5 Very young bats need
  A plenty of sunlight.
  B a cage to live in.
  C a special diet.

Portfolio 5

Write an information page on one of these topics:

- Caring for a particular type of animal
- Choosing a pet for an inner-city home
- An organisation that looks after animals
- Training animals
- Bird watching

Organise your page carefully. Use:

- headings
- lists
- colour, bold, underlining or capital letters to highlight important details

Quiz 5

a What do you remember about Unit 5? Answer all the questions you can and then check in the Student's Book.

A

B

1 What is the opposite of *wild*?

....

2 Fill in the vowels (*a, e, i, o, u*) to make three nouns connected with animals.

spcs ....
snctry ....
srvvl ....

3 Look at picture A. Which animals did this man have a special relationship with?

....

4 Complete this sentence.

RSPCA stands for Royal Society for the Prevention of .... to ....

5 Complete the sentence with the correct words from the box.

though	although	in spite	despite

.... temperatures sometimes reach –14°C, Arctic foxes have a thick coat and they can survive .... the cold.

6 Circle the correct words.

Cats often *burp* / *rub* themselves against your legs. However, if they are angry or scared, they may *scratch* / *chew* you.

7 Which word is the odd one out?

yawn blink burp hiccup

8 Complete the sentence with reflexive pronouns or *each other*.

Sally and Christine had to sit next to 1 ...., but they didn't enjoy 2 .... because they don't like 3 ....

9 Which Spanish organisation looks after the animals in picture B? ....

10 Match the words with the vowel sounds.

1 speak A /ɪə/
2 break B /iː/
3 clear C /e/
4 bread D /eɪ/

b 37 Listen and check your answers.

c Now look at your Student's Book and write three more quiz questions for Unit 5.

Question: ....
....
Answer: ....

Question: ....
....
Answer: ....

Question: ....
....
Answer: ....

6 Take action

1 Vocabulary

Campaigning

a Choose the correct answer: A or B.

1 If someone makes a donation, they
  - **A** give money.
  - **B** give help and support.

2 If you do voluntary work, you
  - **A** raise money for a campaign.
  - **B** don't receive any money for your work.

3 If you want to raise awareness about something, your aim is to
  - **A** understand it better yourself.
  - **B** make it clearer in other people's minds.

4 If someone gives you a flyer, you receive
  - **A** a printed piece of paper.
  - **B** a small amount of money.

5 If an organisation is a charity, it
  - **A** is always supported by the government.
  - **B** aims to help people who need help.

b Complete the texts.

Ban plastic bags!

Join our [1]c.......................... against plastic bags. Help to raise [2]a.......................... about the damage that these bags are causing to the environment. Write to your local supermarket and urge them to take action!

A big thank you to everyone who helped with the school Festival of Comedy last month. Through the [3]v.......................... work of students, parents and teachers, we were able to [4]r.......................... over £2,500, which will go to local charities.

Gillbank Fund

The Gillbank Fund is a [5]c.......................... which helps families who are in difficulties because of illness or poverty. If you are interested in joining our team of helpers, or if you can make a [6]d.......................... to [7]s.......................... our work, please contact us via our website:

www.gillbankfund.org

2 Grammar Grammar reference: page 80

Future review

a Match the sentences with the meanings.

1 I'm going to start my guitar lessons next week. ☐
2 I'll be working at 10 o'clock tomorrow. ☐
3 I think I'll go to bed now. ☐
4 I'll probably pass my exams this year. ☐
5 My girlfriend is meeting me outside the cinema at 7:15. ☐

A This action will already be in progress at that time.
B This is my prediction.
C This is a plan I've already made for the future.
D This is a definite arrangement we've made.
E I've just made this decision about a future action.

b There is a mistake in each of these sentences. ~~Cross out~~ the wrong word(s) and write the correct word(s).

1 Karl and Maria will going to get married in two weeks' time.

....

2 We hope the charity concert will be raising over £1,000.

....

3 What Greg is going to study next year at college?

....

4 You won't be believing the news I've just heard!

....

5 This time tomorrow we'll sit in the bus on our way to the airport.

....

6 Are you cold? I'm going to lend you a jumper if you like.

....

7 I'd like to see Natalie this afternoon. Does she will be working at the supermarket?

....

c Write true answers to the questions. Write full sentences.

1 What are you going to do when you finish this exercise?

....

....

....

2 Do you think you'll get any phone calls this evening? If so, who will call you?

....

....

....

3 What are you going to wear tomorrow?

....

....

....

4 Will you be watching TV at 9:15 tomorrow night? If so, what will you be watching? If not, what will you be doing?

....

....

....

3 Listen

a 38 Listen to two students, Andrew and Nadia. Which topic do they both talk about?

A a charity **B** a campaign **C** a fundraising event

b 38 Listen again. Are the sentences *right* (✓) or *wrong* (✗)?

1 Andrew is supporting a campaign to stop the production of chemicals. ☐

2 Companies that sell fashionable clothes are using factories that pollute the rivers. ☐

3 Andrew believes that the problem of water pollution is getting worse in Asia. ☐

4 He's decided that he isn't going to buy any more jeans or sports clothes. ☐

5 Nadia says that most students at her school are in favour of using bicycles more often for travelling in town. ☐

6 She thinks one of the main problems is that cycle lanes are badly designed. ☐

7 The Green Action Group will be campaigning at the school next weekend. ☐

8 They are hoping that members of the council will support their ideas. ☐

c What do you think of Andrew and Nadia's ideas? Prepare to talk about this in your next class.

4 Vocabulary

Phrasal verbs with *take*

a Complete the sentences with the words in the box.

on	off	up	away	up	down

1 Someone is coming on Friday to bring our new fridge and take .... our old one.
2 If you want to get fit, why don't you take .... running?
3 After the party, we'll have to take .... all these decorations.
4 Their new single has really taken .... It could even reach number one in the charts.
5 Emma does volunteer work at the local youth club. This takes .... a lot of her time.
6 Adam said he wouldn't mind giving me some driving lessons, and I might take him up .... that.

b Replace the underlined words with a phrasal verb with *take*.

1 There are a lot of facts and figures in this article and I couldn't understand it all.
I couldn't .... it all ....
2 I know you're upset, but don't release your anger by being horrible to me.
Don't .... it .... me.
3 Leo started skydiving for the first time last year.
Leo .... skydiving last year.
4 I don't want to have all these magazines on the table. Move them to some other place, please.
.... them .... , please.
5 Since they launched their advertising campaign, the business has started to be very successful.
The business has ....
6 Sara has offered to lend me her rucksack, and I think I'll accept her offer to do that.
I think I'll .... her .... that.
7 That poster doesn't look very good there. I'm going to remove it from the wall.
I'm going to .... it ....
8 We're going to sell the piano. No one uses it and it occupies too much space.
It .... too much space.

Help yourself!

Practice with phrasal verbs

The following sentences contain phrasal verbs that you have seen in Units 1–5. Complete them with the words in the box. If you aren't sure, check in your dictionary.

in	up	down	around	with	out

1 I picked .... a bit of Russian when I was staying in Moscow.
2 You'll need a map to work .... how to get to the village.
3 Slow .... ! You're driving too fast.
4 I wasn't very happy with the decision, but I went along .... it.
5 Joanna sang the first part of the song on her own, and then everyone else joined ....
6 We'll have to find a way to get .... the problem.

5 Grammar Grammar reference: page 80

Future perfect and future perfect continuous

a Write the sentences in the future perfect.

CLOSING DOWN SALE!
21st–23rd September
All clothes at –50% before the shop closes!

1 On 22nd September / the sale / begin
....
....
2 On 20th September / the sale / not start
....
....
3 The shop / close / by the end of September
....
....

CT1107 | ADULT | £43.00
TINA MARTEL AND TRAMWAY FLASH | 7TH APRIL 8:30
TINA MARTEL AND TRAMWAY FLASH
FORUM THEATRE
FRI 7TH APRIL 8:30 PM

4 the band / start / playing by 7 o'clock? / No, it won't.
....
....
5 the concert / take place / by 9th April? / Yes, it will.
....
....

b Complete the sentences with the future perfect continuous form of the verbs.

1 They say this weather will continue until tomorrow night. That means it .... (rain) for five days without stopping!
2 Call me at 10:30 tonight. I won't be tired because I .... (not work) during the afternoon.
3 At 6:00 they'll still be on the train. They .... (travel) for three hours.
4 A: Suzie will probably want to have a good rest on Sunday night.
B: Why? What .... (she / do)?
A: Running in the London Marathon!
5 A: Come on! Annie's already at the cinema.
B: We'll get there in about five minutes, so she .... (not wait) long.
6 A: Patrick's course will be finished at the end of this year.
B: At last! How long .... (he / study) at university?
A: For six years.

c Read the sentences and tick (✓) the correct statement: A or B.

1 *By Thursday I will have written my report.*
A I'll start writing my report on Thursday. ☐
B On Thursday my report will be finished. ☐
2 *Next week his exams will have ended.*
A He won't have any exams next week. ☐
B His exams will finish at the end of next week. ☐
3 *At the end of May, we will have been campaigning for two months.*
A We'll still be campaigning at the end of May. ☐
B Our campaign will be finished before the end of May. ☐
4 *I will have spoken to David by lunch time today.*
A I'm going to speak to David this morning. ☐
B I'll be speaking to David at lunch time. ☐
5 *On 6th July, we will have been living in this flat for two years.*
A We'll still be living here in July. ☐
B We'll stop living here on 6th July. ☐

6 Pronunciation

Elision in future forms

a 39 Listen and tick (✓) the sentence you hear.

1 **A** My parents will be taking a holiday. ☐
B My parents will have taken a holiday. ☐
2 **A** Jane will be staying in Rome for a month. ☐
B Jane will have been staying in Rome for a month. ☐
3 **A** Will you have eaten at the café? ☐
B Will you have been eating at the café? ☐
4 **A** The band will have given a concert. ☐
B The band will have been giving a concert. ☐
5 **A** I'm going to the festival. ☐
B I'm going to go to the festival. ☐
6 **A** Are your friends going to Paris? ☐
B Are your friends going to go to Paris? ☐

b 40 Underline the stressed syllables in these sentences. Then listen, check and repeat.

1 Michael will have left by tomorrow.
2 My cousins will have been using the computer.
3 We will have arrived by six o'clock.
4 They will have been swimming in the river.
5 When will you have finished your lunch?
6 How long will she have been working?

41 Practise saying these words

awareness campaigner donation
focus furniture poverty presentation
publicise supporter voluntary

7 Read

a Read Justin's blog. What is a *gap year*?

A a holiday abroad **B** a break from education
C a student's first year after leaving school
D a period of training for a job

Today it's my 19th birthday and I'm 10,000 kilometres from home. I've just arrived in South Africa, and I'll be doing voluntary work at a hospital here for the next five weeks.

When I passed my final exams last year, I decided to take a 'gap year', travelling and working before I take up my university studies. I wanted to do something to help people, so I arranged to come to this children's hospital near Cape Town. There are six volunteers here at the moment. We have no medical training, but that isn't important – our role will be to organise activities for the children, to bring some fun and laughter into their lives while they're going through a hard time in hospital. I know it won't be easy. I'll be working for six hours a day from Monday to Friday and the work will take imagination, patience and lots of energy. But it will also be rewarding and I hope that by the end of my time here I will have helped to make life happier for some of the children.

At the weekends I'll be able to catch a train into Cape Town for a bit of shopping and sightseeing, but I'm going to spend most of my free time at the fantastic beaches here. I've already arranged to go surfing with some of the other volunteers next Saturday and I've also decided to try ocean kayaking and windsurfing.

When I leave the hospital I'm going to meet up with my friend Javier in Johannesburg, where he will have been staying for a week, and we're going to travel up through Africa together. We haven't got a fixed schedule, but we definitely want to see some African wildlife and we also want to climb Mount Kilimanjaro. Eventually we'll get to Morocco and we're going take a ferry to Spain. Javier's uncle lives near Seville and he's going to give us some work picking fruit so we can earn some money.

When I get back to the UK, I think I will have had a fantastic adventure. I will have been living and travelling independently and experiencing life in places very different from the world I know. I hope I will have made new friends along the way, and I know I will have learnt a lot. You can follow my progress on this blog!

b Choose the correct answer: A, B or C.

1 Next year Justin will be
  A going back to school.
  B starting a course at university.
  C continuing his university studies.

2 During the next five weeks he will be
  A working at the hospital seven days a week.
  B helping the doctors at the hospital.
  C entertaining children at the hospital.

3 In his free time he is going to
  A spend a lot of time shopping.
  B take up some new water sports.
  C meet a friend in Johannesburg.

4 When Justin leaves the hospital
  A Javier will already have arrived in Africa.
  B he and Javier will have been travelling together.
  C he will have gone mountain climbing with Javier.

5 The two boys are planning
  A to go to Morocco by ferry.
  B to look for a job in Spain.
  C to earn some money before they go home.

6 When Justin gets home he
  A will be having a wonderful experience.
  B will probably make some new friends.
  C will have been writing about his travels in his blog.

Portfolio 6

Write your own blog entry on the subject of *The next twelve months*. Write one paragraph about yourself and one paragraph about another person. Think about these ideas:

- definite plans or intentions
  I'm/He's going to …
- predictions
  (I think) I'll/she'll (probably) …
  I/He might …
- conditions and achievements in a year's time
  In a year's time I'll/she'll be …
  By (date) *I'll/he will have …*

Quiz 6

a What do you remember about Unit 6? Answer all the questions you can and then check in the Student's Book.

A

B

1 **What is the person doing in picture A? Complete the sentence.**

He's m.................... a d.............................. .

2 **Match the words to make three collocations.**

1 raise — A flyers
2 support — B awareness
3 give out — C a charity

3 **What is Manpreet Darroch's campaign about? Put the letters in order.**

dora fetyas ....

4 **What is the UK charity event in picture B?**

....

5 **Circle the correct verbs.**

A: *I'll visit* / *I'm going to visit* Rachel in hospital tomorrow. I hope *she's going to feel* / *she'll be feeling* better then.

B: That's a good idea. *I'll come* / *I'll be coming* with you.

6 **Complete the sentence with words from the box.**

in off on up down away

He took .... acting two years ago and since then his career has really taken ....

7 **Put the words in order to make a sentence.**

going to / to help me / take / your offer / you / I'm / on / up

....

....

8 **Read the sentence. Are the following statements *right* (✓) or *wrong* (✗)?**

They will have arrived by the time we get home.

A We'll get home before they arrive. ☐
B They'll get home at the same time as us. ☐
C They'll be at home when we get there. ☐

9 **Complete the sentence.**

He'll be tired this evening. He .... training at the pool all afternoon.

10 **Underline the stressed syllables in this sentence.**

Emma will have been working in the library.

b 42 Listen and check your answers.

c Now look at your Student's Book and write three more quiz questions for Unit 6.

Question: ....
....
Answer: ....

Question: ....
....
Answer: ....

Question: ....
....
Answer: ....

7 Self-image

1 Vocabulary

Describing clothes and materials

a Look at the table: 1 is S, 3 is P and 6 is T. Write all these letters in the puzzle. Then complete the adjectives for clothes and write the letters in the table.

1	2	3	4	5	6	7	8	9	10
S		P			T				

11	12	13	14	15	16	17	18	19	20

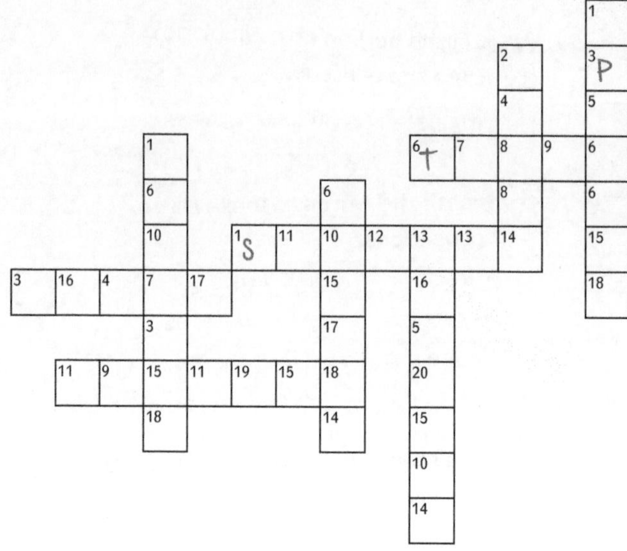

b Two adjectives are wrong in each of these sentences. Look at the pictures, ~~cross out~~ the wrong adjectives and write the correct ones.

1 She's wearing a spotted skirt and a plain, long-sleeved T-shirt.

....

2 He always wears tight jeans and today he's wearing a checked T-shirt under a short jacket.

....

3 Today she's wearing a pair of old plain trousers and she looks quite trendy.

....

2 Grammar Grammar reference: page 88

Passive review

a Circle the correct words.

1 Some of the world's best perfume *produced / is produced* in France.

2 Prizes *will / will be* given for the most creative dress designs.

3 Some valuable paintings have been *stolen / stealing* from the museum.

4 Trousers weren't *worn / wore* by women in the 19th century.

5 When *are / were* sunglasses invented?

6 Has your brother *be / been* taught to swim?

b Make six sentences from the table.

Jean-Paul Gaultier's fashion show	is	built	in the future.
This shirt	are	solved	last month in Paris.
I hope this problem	was	published	about 4,500 years ago.
More than 200,000 new books	were	made	since the 16th century.
The Egyptian Pyramids	have been	grown	of cotton.
In South America, olive trees	will be	held	every year in the UK.

1 ....

....

2 ....

....

3 ....

....

4 ....

....

5 ....

....

6 ....

....

c 43 Complete the dialogues with the correct passive form of the verbs. Then listen and check.

A: That's a really nice bag.
B: Yes, it [1] .... (make) of Italian leather and it [2] .... (design) by Prada in Milan. You should go to the Bag Boutique. All their prices [3] .... (reduce) yesterday.
A: Really? I might go and have a look. I'm getting paid tomorrow, so I'll have some money to spend!

A: I haven't heard that song before.
B: No, it [4] .... just .... (release). They recorded it last year but it [5] .... (not include) on their album. It's good, isn't it?
A: Yeah, I like it.
B: Their songs [6] .... usually .... (write) by the lead guitarist, but this one's really old. It was originally a jazz song that [7] .... (record) in the 1930s.

Help yourself!

Modal verbs in the passive

Other modal verbs, as well as *will*, can be used in the passive. The form is:

- modal + *be* + past participle to refer to the present and future

  This jumper ***can be washed*** *in warm water.*

  The concert ***might be held*** *next July.*

- modal + *have been* + past participle to refer to the past

  The problem with the TV ***may have been caused*** *by the storm yesterday.*

Complete the sentences in the passive.

1 Safety helmets .... (must / wear) on the building site.
2 This ring .... (might / make) of gold, but I'm not sure.
3 They told us the new fridge .... (would / deliver) next Monday.
4 The guitar I wanted wasn't in the shop. It .... (must / sell) last week.
5 Why is the rubbish still here? It .... (should / take) away yesterday.

3 Read

a Read the article. What is the main topic? Choose the correct answer.

A the latest fashions for pop stars
B new technology in the fashion world
C the use of LEDs in clothing
D problems with 'wearable technology'

Switched-on style:
the brighter side of fashion

Pop star Katy Perry lit up the room in 2010 when she appeared in New York in a dress that shone in different colours, and in the following year she made headlines in a costume covered with thousands of coloured lights for a TV performance of her single *E.T.* Around the same time, The NYC Boys, a Japanese superstar band, and the singer Safura also performed in clothes that magically changed colour and pattern [1]............... .

All these outfits were created by CuteCircuit, a London company that aims to bring together the latest technology and traditional fashion design. The light effects were produced by using LEDs – tiny devices that send out light [2]............... . An amazing silk creation called the 'Galaxy Dress' was made by the same company in 2009 and is displayed in the Museum of Science and Industry in Chicago. Its 24,000 LEDs are powered by small iPod batteries and they produce an effect that is like a waterfall of light and colour.

Clothing with built-in electronics has been around for some time, [3]............... – for example, the clothes with devices that measure an athlete's performance or heart rate. But now high-tech clothing is taking off in the fashion world, and these new garments are not only for pop stars and museums. Whether you're a man or a woman, you can now buy clothes that light up and change colour as you move, with batteries that can be recharged from your computer. Designers are experimenting with clothing made of solar panels, and already there are solar-powered jackets and swimsuits [4]............... . There is even a dress that operates as a mobile phone – the phone card fits into the label at the back, the microphone is at the wrist [5]............... .

Combining the very different skills of technical engineers and fashion designers isn't easy, and the high cost of production remains a problem. But it's an exciting field which is just opening up. In the future we can expect spectacular developments in 'wearable technology' [6]............... .

The Galaxy Dress

b Read the article again and put the phrases (A–F) in the correct places (1–6).

A especially in sportswear
B and a call is made just by raising your arm
C when electricity is passed through them
D which may completely change the way we think about clothes
E in response to their movements
F that can be used to charge up your phone or iPod

c What other examples of 'wearable technology' can you think of, and what is your opinion of them? Prepare to talk about this in your next class.

4 Pronunciation

Intrusive /j/, /r/ and /w/

a 44 Listen and tick (✓) the extra sound you hear between the underlined words. Then listen again and repeat.

	/j/	/w/	/r/
1 How is your mother?	☐	☐	☐
2 They might be outside.	☐	☐	☐
3 Go away!	☐	☐	☐
4 Where are you?	☐	☐	☐
5 Do you know Anna and Jane?	☐	☐	☐
6 It's a funny advertisement.	☐	☐	☐
7 Did you open the door?	☐	☐	☐
8 I saw Andrew this morning.	☐	☐	☐

Check it out!

The word *the* is usually pronounced /ðə/. However, before a word starting with a vowel it is pronounced /ði/ and a /j/ sound is added between the two words.

the man /ðə mæn/
the old man /ðijəuld mæn/

b 45 Listen and practise saying these sentences.

He's the owner of the Indian restaurant.
Her new anorak is blue and white.
Where are Alice and Paul? Are they outside?
I'm going for another interview on Monday.
My aunt is flying to Canada and the USA.

46 Practise saying these words

casual cheerful enthusiastic flowery
influence neutral old-fashioned pattern
possession sensation striped violent

5 Grammar Grammar reference: page 88

have / get something done

a Match the two parts of the sentences.

1 My parents are having the living room ☐
2 Our roof is leaking. We'll have to get it ☐
3 He's just had his hair ☐
4 I'm going to have my teeth ☐
5 They should get all that rubbish ☐
6 They had lots of photos ☐

A repaired.
B taken at their wedding.
C checked by the dentist.
D cut.
E redecorated.
F taken away.

b Complete the sentences. Use the verbs in the box and the words in brackets.

get / repair have / clean get / test
have / wash get / deliver have / paint

1 She's .... (her hair)

2 We need to .... (the TV)

3 They .... last night. (some pizzas)

4 He's just .... (his jacket)

5 Our neighbours are .... (their house)

6 She .... yesterday. (her eyes)

6 Vocabulary

Body idioms

a Use the pictures to complete the expressions.

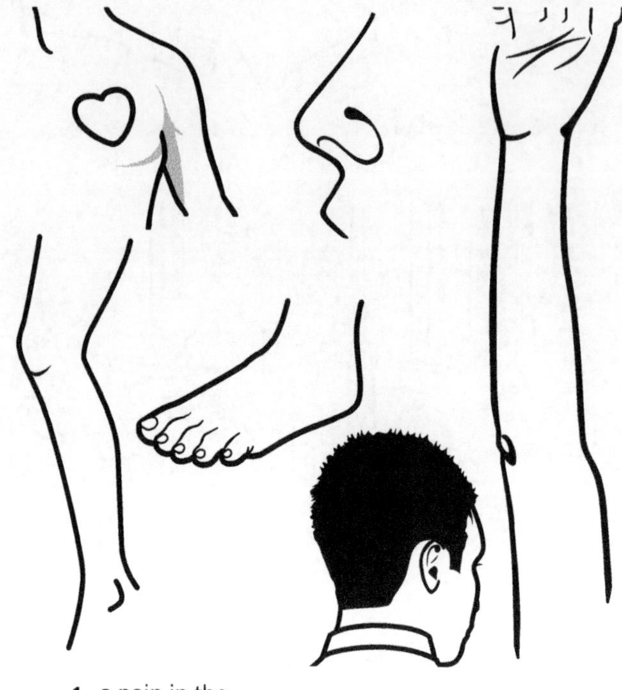

1 a pain in the ....
2 put your .... in it
3 set your .... on something
4 a ....y person
5 pull someone's ....
6 from head to ....
7 a big-..................ed person
8 cost an .... and a ....

b Complete the sentences with expressions from Exercise 6a.

1 She doesn't talk much about her achievements – she doesn't want to seem ....
2 I .... when I asked about Eva's boyfriend. She looked really embarrassed, but I didn't mean to upset her.
3 Who can afford to buy these cars? They ....
4 He's .... on getting into the national team. He'll be terribly disappointed if he doesn't make it.
5 James keeps annoying me. He's a ....
6 Hey, stop trying to read my emails – they're private. Don't be so ....
7 A: You can't be serious!
B: No, no. I was just ....
8 The mosquitoes were terrible! We were covered in bites ....

7 Listen

a 47 Listen to the interview about fashions of the past. Which picture shows the period they are discussing?

b 47 Listen again and complete each sentence with <u>one</u> word.

1 Young people wanted to forget the horrors of the .... that had just ended.
2 Before this period, women's bodies were .... by long dresses.
3 'Flappers' wore dresses that ended at the ....
4 The trendy hairstyles for women were very ....
5 The cloche was a type of ....
6 Men's baggy trousers were .... up at the bottom.
7 Men put oil on their ....
8 Knickerbockers were short .... that were worn by men.

Portfolio 7

Write an article for a website on one of these topics:

- Celebrities' fashions at a recent event
- Costumes in a recent film or TV show
- The fashions of a particular time in the past

Include:

- a description of the clothing that was worn (styles, colours, materials)
- a description of hairstyles and accessories (e.g. hats, jewellery, bags)
- your opinion of the 'look' that was achieved

Add photos or drawings if you wish.

Quiz 7

a What do you remember about Unit 7? Answer all the questions you can and then check in the Student's Book.

1 Circle the odd one out.

tight trendy smart fashionable

2 Look at picture A and complete the sentence.

She's wearing a short-.................... top with a .... scarf, and she's holding a .... umbrella.

3 Put the letters in order and make two words for patterns.

pirsedt ....

welfroy ....

4 There are two mistakes in this sentence. Write the correct sentence.

The film is made two years ago, but it still hasn't released as a DVD.

....

....

5 Complete the sentences with the passive form of the verbs.

Several buildings .... (damage) by the fire last night. I hope they .... (can / repair).

6 Look at picture B. Put the letters in the correct order to complete the sentence.

He's got a .... *(ottato)*, a .... *(nercipig)* and a lot of .... *(werlyjeel)*.

(A) (B)

7 Put the words in order to make a sentence.

designed / their / They're / architect / by / having / an / house

....

....

8 Circle the correct word.

Designer clothes cost an *arm* / *ear* / *eye* and a *foot* / *leg* / *head*.

9 What does the sentence mean? Choose the correct answer: A, B or C.

I think she's a pain in the neck.

A I think her neck is sore. ☐

B I think she's very upset. ☐

C I think she's really annoying. ☐

10 Look at the underlined letters. Match them with the extra sounds that go between them.

1 I'm so unhappy!	**A** /w/
2 Austria and Poland	**B** /j/
3 She isn't here.	**C** /r/

b 48 Listen and check your answers.

c Now look at your Student's Book and write three more quiz questions for Unit 7.

Question: ....

....

Answer: ....

Question: ....

....

Answer: ....

Question: ....

....

Answer: ....

8 Something for nothing

1 Grammar Grammar reference: page 90

Third conditional review

a Read each sentence and then decide if the following statement is *right* (✓) or *wrong* (✗).

1 *If I'd had more time, I would have phoned you for a chat this morning.*
I phoned you for a chat this morning. ☐

2 *You would have enjoyed last night's quiz show if you'd watched it.*
You didn't watch the quiz show last night. ☐

3 *If they hadn't worked in the summer, they would have needed to borrow some money.*
They had jobs in the summer, so they didn't need to borrow any money. ☐

4 *Steve wouldn't have lost the tickets if he'd kept them in his wallet.*
Steve kept the tickets in his wallet so he wouldn't lose them. ☐

5 *If we'd known about the problem, we may have been able to help.*
Maybe we could have helped, but we didn't know about the problem. ☐

6 *I might not have heard about the free concert if Amy hadn't told me.*
I didn't find out about the concert from Amy. ☐

b Write the sentences in the third conditional.

1 Chris / do / more research – he / write / a better essay

....

....

2 I / finish / the cleaning by now – you / give / me a hand

....

....

3 we / arrive / earlier – the train / not be / late

....

....

4 you / see / Luisa in her costume – you / not recognise / her

....

....

5 how / we / get / here – we / not have / a map?

....

....

c Use your own ideas to complete the sentences.

1 If I hadn't been at school last Friday, ...
....

2 ....
.... if I'd had enough money.

3 If..
.............................., it would have been brilliant!

4 It would have been a disaster for me if ....
....

2 Vocabulary

Phrasal verbs and expressions with *give*

a Circle the correct words.

1 Do you need some help with that? I can give you *a hand / a go* if you like.
2 Maria's very generous. She gives a lot of her money *out / away* to charity.
3 I'll lend you my jacket, but you'll have to give it *in / back* to me tomorrow.
4 What do you think of this painting? Give me your *hand / opinion*.
5 It's a very challenging job. You won't succeed unless you give it *out / your all*.
6 I'm getting a motorcycle! For ages my parents refused to let me have one, but they've finally given *in / away*.
7 They were giving *out / off* flyers to publicise the concert.
8 I don't know if I'll be able to play this on the guitar, but I'll give it *a go / an opinion*.

b 49 Complete the expressions in the dialogues. Then listen and check.

A: Hey Simon, will you give me a [1] ....?
I want to move the piano to the other side of the room, and there's no way I can do it on my own.
B: Well, OK, we can give it [2] ...., but I think it'll be too heavy for two people.
A: We'll do it! Come on – give [3] .... all.
B: Oh no! That's impossible, Matt.
A: OK, I give [4] .... We'll have to wait until my brothers get home.

A: I really want to lose some weight now.
B: If you're serious about that, I think you should give up sweets and chocolates.
A: Stop eating chocolates? No way! I can't do that!
B: Well, it's your choice, but I've given you my [5] .... You eat too much sugary food.
A: Yeah. I know you're right really. But Mike gave me this lovely box of chocolates yesterday. What am I going to do with it? I can't give it [6] .... to him. That would hurt his feelings.
B: So take the chocolates to school. You can give them [7] .... to everyone in your class.
A: Yes, I guess that's a good idea.

Help yourself!

Verbs with two objects

Look at the examples. In the second sentence, *give* has two objects: *the books* and *Carlo* or *him*. The form is *give* + indirect object (person) + direct object (noun).

I gave the books to Carlo/him.
I gave Carlo/him the books.

The direct object must be a noun. If it is a pronoun, we don't use this form.

I gave them to Carlo/him. ~~*I gave Carlo/him them.*~~

Some other verbs can be used in the same way, e.g. *make, buy, show, send, bring, take, lend, offer.*

Are these sentences *right* (✓) or *wrong* (✗)?

1 When we saw Ellie, we showed her the photos. ☐
2 I took my aunt some flowers when she was in hospital. ☐
3 Will you make for me a sandwich? ☐
4 Josh found the website address and sent us it. ☐
5 It's Dad's birthday soon. I've bought some gloves for him. ☐
6 I lent Hana some magazines and she's forgotten to give me them back. ☐

3 Grammar Grammar reference: page 86

Expressions of purpose, reason and result

a Match the two parts of the sentences.

1 She got up early so as ☐
2 Mum uses this little gadget for ☐
3 She switched off her computer so that ☐
4 Maria has gone to the shops to ☐
5 Our neighbour has injuries due to ☐
6 She left the building at about 6:30, so ☐

A falling down the steps.
B to catch the 7:15 train.
C it was dark by the time she got home.
D look for some new sports shoes.
E it wouldn't waste energy.
F cleaning her keyboard.

b Choose the correct answer: A, B or C.

1 I've almost run out of money now, ... I'll have to find a cash machine.
A so B so that C so as

2 They started selling eggs and vegetables at the market in order .... some money.
A they could earn B for earning C to earn

3 There are two different instructions on this packet. .... it's confusing.
A Due to B Therefore,
C As a result of

4 We're going to donate some food and clothing .... help the victims of the earthquake.
A for B for to C to

5 Type in your date of birth and your security number so as .... your bank account.
A accessing B to access
C you can access

6 Flights from Heathrow Airport were delayed this morning due to ....
A the bad weather B being bad weather
C the weather was bad

c Complete the sentences so that the meaning is the same. Use the word(s) in brackets.

1 He went to the supermarket for some cheese. (buy)
He went ....
....

2 Because we wanted to save time, we decided to call a taxi.
(so as)
We decided ....
....

3 The cost of living has gone up as a result of the high price of petrol.
(due)
The cost of living ....
....

4 I wanted to get some new sunglasses, so I borrowed £10 from my sister.
(so that / could)
I borrowed ....
....
....

5 There has been a big increase in population and therefore the city is overcrowded.
(result of)
The city is ....
....
....

4 Vocabulary

Numbers and symbols

a Write these expressions as numbers and symbols.

1 twenty-eight kilograms ....
2 seventy-two percent ....
3 nineteen degrees ....
4 eighty-six point oh one three ....
5 minus forty-five ....
6 three – nil ....
7 eight thousand two hundred and fourteen dollars ....
8 the twenty-fifth of December, two thousand and twelve ....
9 six million, four hundred and ninety-one thousand, seven hundred and one ....

Check it out!

Look at these examples for ways of saying 0.

- We say *zero* or *nought* for the number on its own.
Five times zero equals zero.
- We usually say *oh* in phone numbers. For 00 we say *double oh*.
0135 412 009: *oh one three five, four one two, double oh nine*
- We say *oh* or *zero* in other long number sequences and in decimals after the point.
Account no. 560210: *five six oh two one oh*
30.408: *thirty point four oh eight*
- We say *nil* for football scores.
Arsenal beat Liverpool 2–0: *two – nil*

b Write the words for the symbols and numbers in grey.

1 248 + 67 = 315 ....
2 77 – 58 = 19 ....
3 380 ÷ 4 = 95 ....
4 62 + 39 = 101 ....
5 40kg ....
6 98.3% ....
7 32° ....
8 50% ....
9 12 – (3 x 4) = 0 ....
10 date: 31 /7/2014 ....

5 Pronunciation

Large numbers

Check it out!

There are no fixed rules for saying phone numbers. However, this is a common pattern:

- Say the area code all together without a pause.
- Say the rest in groups of three or four numbers.

a 50 Listen and write the phone numbers. Leave a space where you hear a pause. Then listen again, check and repeat.

1 ....
2 ....
3 ....
4 ....
5 ....
6 ....

b 51 Say these phrases with large numbers. Then listen, check and repeat.

£6,758　　138,420 km
$12,914　　10,573,139 people
€362,802

c Practise saying these numbers in English.

- your phone number
- a friend's phone number
- your date of birth
- your postcode
- your bank card number if you have one

52 Practise saying these words

alternative　appointment　appreciate
donate　edible　experiment　officially
relationship　service　warrior

6 Listen

a 53 Listen and match the recordings (1–5) with the situations (A–G). There are two extra situations.

1 ☐　2 ☐　3 ☐　4 ☐　5 ☐

A talking about a bank account
B asking about a train service
C giving information at a station
D advertising to customers in a shop
E commenting on a football match
F giving a news report
G finding out how to contact someone

b 53 Listen again and write the numbers you hear.

1 a usual price: £..........
b today's price: £..........
2 a phone number: ....
b mobile number: ....
3 a account number: ....
b amount of money: £..........
4 a score in previous match: ....
b number of spectators: ....
5 a normal departure time: ....
b today's departure time: ....

7 Read

a Read the text and find the correct place (1–4) for the headings. There are two extra headings.

A Earning and saving **B** Expectations **C** Spending
D Bank accounts **E** Changes due to the economy
F Lending and borrowing

Money survey

A recent survey has investigated the way American teenagers aged 16–18 relate to money – what they do with it, how they are affected by the recent financial problems in the world and what they expect in the future. The results make interesting reading.

1 ....
Of those surveyed, almost all have a mobile phone and more than three-quarters have an iPod or MP3 player. 66% own a computer, 46% own a TV and 27% own a car. However, most of their own money is spent on clothes. Three out of four teens reported that they have bought new clothes in the past three months, and for girls this figure was much higher (86%). If they were given the choice, 63% said they would choose a new pair of jeans rather than tickets to a concert, and 75% would choose a new pair of shoes rather than 50 new MP3 downloads.

2 ....
Over two-thirds of these young people do some form of work in order to earn money. The average earnings are $1,630 per year, with boys earning more than girls. Most teens also save money – they are usually saving up for clothes, a piece of technology, future university expenses or a car. Only 21% of teens are not saving at all. However, if they were given $500, over half of those surveyed said they would spend the money rather than saving it.

3 ....
The world has been hit hard by financial problems lately and 93% of the teens said that this had affected them and their family. Most of them are finding that they have less to spend and therefore they are shopping more carefully. 55% wait for items to go on sale at reduced prices and 42% do research to compare prices and choose the best deals. Sales of tech gadgets to teens remain strong, but spending on expensive clothing has dropped. More teens are shopping in cheaper stores and looking for second-hand bargains, while some are starting to make their own clothes.

4 ....
Many teenagers are worried about rising university costs and the difficulty of finding jobs. However, 59% still believe they will be in a better financial position than their parents in the future. At the same time, 65% expect that their choice of career will be based on their passion for the job, while only 15% think it will depend on how much money they can earn.

b Read the text again and choose the correct answer: A, B or C.

1 The survey was conducted
   A by teenagers.
   B in the USA.
   C due to financial problems.

2 In the past three months, 75 per cent of the teenagers have bought
   A new clothes.
   B new shoes.
   C an iPod or MP3 player.

3 The survey found that boys … than girls.
   A are more likely to have a job
   B get more money from their work
   C save more money

4 As a result of problems in the economy, teenagers
   A aren't saving much money.
   B don't go shopping very often.
   C shop more carefully than they used to.

5 Recently, fewer teenagers have been
   A buying high-tech equipment.
   B buying expensive clothes.
   C spending money in cheaper shops.

6 Almost sixty per cent of the teenagers think that in the future
   A they will have more money than their parents.
   B it will be difficult to get a job.
   C money will be the most important thing when they choose a job.

Portfolio 8

Write four questions for your own survey about money. Include some conditional questions, for example:

If …, *which would you choose/prefer?*
what would you spend the money on?
what would you have done?

Provide three alternatives for people to choose from.

Interview at least five people. Then write a report on your findings.

Quiz 8

a What do you remember about Unit 8? Answer all the questions you can and then check in the Student's Book.

1 **Look at picture A and choose the sentence that is not true.**

A He never uses money to buy things.
B He doesn't use any electricity.
C He grows his own fruit and vegetables.
D He has written a book about his experiences.

2 **Does the contraction *'d* mean *had* or *would*?**

If [1]I'd known the answer, [2]I'd have given it to you.

1 .... 2 ....

3 **Complete the third conditional sentence with the correct form of the verbs.**

Sam .... (buy) that video game if he .... (have) enough money.

4 **Look at picture B and write the third conditional sentence.**

she / not hurt / her foot – she / be / able to play basketball

....

....

5 **Circle the odd one out.**

give delay donate provide

6 **Circle the correct word.**

I've given *in* / *away* / *out* all my old toys to a charity for children.

7 **Complete the sentence. Choose words from the box.**

back	out	my all	a go	a hand	an opinion

The teacher was giving .... sports equipment to everyone and she asked me to give her ....

8 **Read the sentence and tick (✓) the correct statement(s).**

We went to the café to see Nicole.

A We went to the café so as to see Nicole. ☐
B We went to the café so we saw Nicole. ☐
C We went to the café as a result of seeing Nicole. ☐
D We went to the café so that we could see Nicole. ☐

9 **Write the numbers.**

A Fifteen times three equals ....
B Three plus nought point five equals ....

10 **Are the following sentences *right* (✓) or *wrong* (✗)?**

A Twenty-five per cent means a quarter. ☐
B Fifty multiplied by two is twenty-five. ☐
C Minus twenty-five degrees is colder than minus thirty. ☐
D 25/4/2010 was the twenty-fifth of April. ☐

b 54 Listen and check your answers.

c Now look at your Student's Book and write three more quiz questions for Unit 8.

Question: ....
....
Answer: ....

Question: ....
....
Answer: ....

Question: ....
....
Answer: ....

9 Keep your cool

1 Vocabulary

Adjectives of character

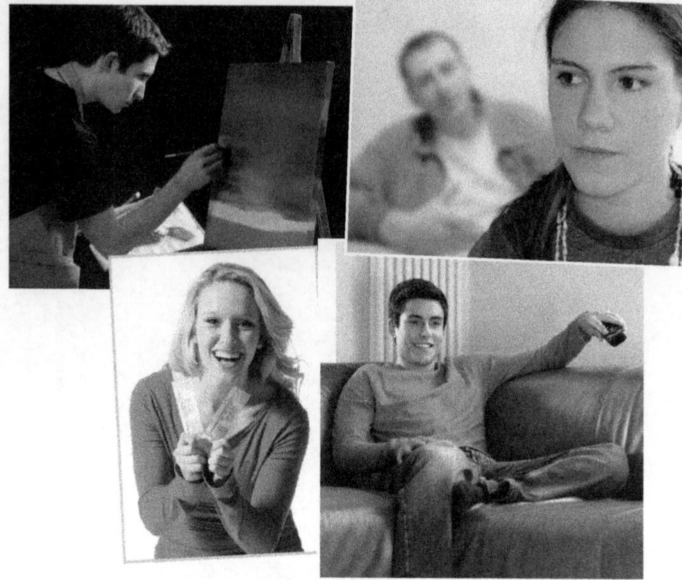

a Look at the table: 1 is E, 6 is S and 14 is G. Write all these letters in the puzzle. Then complete the adjectives of character and write the letters in the table.

1	2	3	4	5	6	7	8	9	10
E					S				

11	12	13	14	15	16	17	18	19
			G					

Across:
- 1(E) 2 3 4 5 6(S) 7 8 6 3 7 9
- 11 1 8 12 13 5 6
- 6 3 5 15 15 13 16 2
- 6 10 8 16 3
- 16 1 15 1 12 12 7 13 5 6
- 9 4 1 1 16 19 5 12

Down:
- 7 10 8 14(G) 7 2 8 3 7 18 1
- 6 17 13 7 12 3
- 16 1 12 7 8 15 12 1
- 8 14 14 16 1 6 6 7 18 1

b Complete the sentences with adjectives from Exercise 1a.

1. Alicia has unusual and wonderful ideas. She's very ....
2. Emily is .... because she thinks Tom likes you more than her.
3. An .... person is always ready to attack or argue with other people.
4. You can always depend on Ryan. He's completely ....
5. Kasim is .... about having a fancy dress party. He thinks it's a great idea.
6. Nothing seems to annoy or depress Daniela. She's always ....

c Write the opposites of these adjectives.

1. reliable ....
2. polite ....
3. friendly ....
4. responsible ....
5. respectful ....

Help yourself!

Adjective endings

The table below shows some of the most common adjective endings. Make adjectives from the nouns and write them in the table. Then check the words and their spelling in your dictionary.

success flower poison volcano pain competition fashion ambition romance silk protection value

-ive	*-ic*
1	7 ....
2	8 ....
-ous	***-able***
3	9 ....
4	10 ....
-ful	***-y***
5	11 ....
6	12 ....

2 Grammar Grammar reference: page 92

should, ought to and *had better*

a Circle the correct words.

1 People shouldn't *park / to park* their cars in front of the garage.
2 *We / We'd* better close the windows before we go out.
3 You should *try / trying* to be more patient with your sister.
4 Everyone ought *understand / to understand* that recycling is important.
5 It's time Lisa *learns / learned* how to swim properly.
6 *You hadn't better / You'd better not* leave your bike here. It isn't safe.

b Use your own ideas to complete the sentences.

1 Emily keeps getting bad headaches. She should ....
2 Jenny and Liam are always arguing. They ought ....
3 Pete is twenty years old now. It's time he ....
4 It's getting very late. You shouldn't ....
5 The baby is asleep now. We'd better not ....

3 Vocabulary

Expressions for arguments

a Use words from both boxes to make expressions for arguments. Write them in the correct list.

keep   lose your   see someone's   lose
keep your   wind   storm   get on

point of view   it   your nerves   the peace
someone up   temper   cool   out

You're extremely angry
1 You ....
2 You ....
3 You ....

People or things annoy you
4 They ....

You want to annoy somebody
5 You ....

You stop other people from arguing
6 You ....

You don't get angry
7 You ....
8 You ....

b 55 There are two mistakes in each of these dialogues. ~~Cross out~~ the two wrong words and write the correct words. Then listen and check.

A: Tony's always teasing me about my curly hair. It really puts on my nerves.
B: Well, don't react! Try to keep the cool. He's just trying to wind you up.

1 .... 2 ....

A: What happened? Where's Adam?
B: Oh, when I told him I'd broken his sunglasses, he really lost them. He shouted at me for about three minutes and then he stormed away.

3 .... 4 ....

A: My mum keeps ringing me to find out what I'm doing. She seems to think I'm still about twelve years old! Sometimes it's hard not to keep my temper with her.
B: Yeah, I know, but try to see her paint of view. She gets worried when she doesn't know where you are.

5 .... 6 ....

4 Read

a Read the text. Who is the article written for? Tick (✓) the correct answer(s).

children ☐ teenagers ☐ parents ☐
step-parents and grandparents ☐

Behaviour contracts for teenagers

If conflict between you and your son or daughter is a problem, maybe it's time you thought about setting up a 'home rules contract'. This is an idea that's being used more and more often, especially in families with rebellious teenage children. We interviewed Dr Amy Barker, a psychologist, who is in favour of the idea.

What is a home rules contract?
Dr Barker: It's a formal agreement about the rules of behaviour that teenagers are expected to follow at home. It should state clearly what the rules are, what privileges the teens will get if they obey the rules and what punishments will follow if they don't. The contract is signed by everyone involved, just like a legal document.

Who ought to write the contract?
Dr Barker: All the adults who have a parental role should be involved – these may include divorced parents, step-parents or grandparents. It's important that they all agree and stick to the rules themselves. At the same time, the teenagers should also contribute their ideas. If they take part in making the rules, they'll be more likely to follow them. The final contract ought to be the result of discussion, respecting everyone's point of view, and all the people who have signed should get a copy.

What are the advantages of a contract?
Dr Barker: It makes it very clear to teens what they can and can't do, and they can see what the consequences of their actions will be. So they learn to control their behaviour. For parents, the contract strengthens their authority and helps them to be fair and reliable.

What areas should be covered in a contract?
Dr Barker: That depends. You can't make rules for everything, so you have to decide what's most important and where the main problems lie. Common topics include the hours when teenagers ought to be home, the spending money they receive, the chores they are expected to do at home and their use of phones or networking sites. For older teens, rules about driving a car may also be important.

Do contracts solve all the problems?
Dr Barker: No, of course not! There will always be conflicts and disagreements between people in a family. But a contract that everyone respects can help to keep the peace.

b Find words in the text for these definitions.

1 serious disagreement or fighting between people (paragraph 1)
....
2 special rights or advantages (paragraph 2)
....
3 to do what you are told to do (paragraph 2)
....
4 to give, for a purpose that is shared with other people (paragraph 3)
....
5 results that follow an action (paragraph 4)
....
6 makes (something) stronger (paragraph 4)
....

c Circle the correct words.

1 Dr Barker has a *positive / negative* opinion of home rules contracts.
2 The contract *is / isn't* a legal document.
3 Dr Barker says that teenagers *ought to / have to* participate in making the rules in the contract.
4 She believes that a contract helps teenagers to *see other people's point of view / control their behaviour.*
5 She gives examples of things that *should / may* be included in a contract.

d What do you think of the idea of a 'home rules contract'? Would it work? Would it be helpful? Prepare to talk about this in your next lesson.

5 Grammar Grammar reference: page 92

Expressing wishes and regrets

a Read each sentence and then decide if the statement below is *right* (✓) or *wrong* (✗).

1 *I wish they would stop making that noise.*
They aren't making a noise now. ☐

2 *If only we had a torch!*
Unfortunately, we didn't have a torch. ☐

3 *I shouldn't have lost my temper.*
I'm sorry I lost my temper. ☐

4 *If only Luke had sent me a message!*
I hope I'll get a message from Luke. ☐

5 *I wish Nicole wasn't so stubborn.*
Nicole is a very stubborn person. ☐

6 *I wish the bus would come.*
The bus isn't here – I want it to come soon. ☐

b Write two sentences for each picture.

1 If only it / stop / raining
I shouldn't / leave / my umbrella at home

....

....

....

2 I wish we / have / some coffee
You should / buy / a packet yesterday

....

....

....

3 I wish I / know / where Anna is
If only she / call / me

....

....

....

4 I wish I / not catch / this train
If only it / not be / so crowded

....

....

....

c Complete the sentences, using your own ideas.

1 It's so cold today! If only ....
....!

2 Stefan was late for his interview. He should
....

3 Hana is still angry with me. I wish ....
....

4 I'd love to go to that concert. I wish ....
....

5 Their car was far too expensive. They shouldn't
....

6 Pronunciation

Unstressed vowel sounds /ə/ and /ɪ/

a 56 Underline the stressed syllable in these words. Then listen and tick (✓) /ə/ or /ɪ/ for the unstressed syllable. Listen again and repeat.

	/ə/	/ɪ/		/ə/	/ɪ/
award	☐	☐	feature	☐	☐
damage	☐	☐	reduce	☐	☐
control	☐	☐	neutral	☐	☐
delay	☐	☐	decide	☐	☐

b 57 These words contain both /ə/ and /ɪ/ for the unstressed syllables. Underline the stressed syllable. Then write 1 and 2 to show the order of the two unstressed syllables. Listen, check and repeat.

	/ə/	/ɪ/		/ə/	/ɪ/
protective	☐	☐	amazing	☐	☐
furniture	☐	☐	punishment	☐	☐
researcher	☐	☐	delicious	☐	☐
hurricane	☐	☐	advantage	☐	☐

c 58 Listen and practise saying these sentences.

Polish and Russian are difficult languages.
It's a delicious way of cooking chicken.
She was very nervous about the hurricane.
David was expecting to become a musician.
I received an urgent message from Elizabeth.

59 Practise saying these words

acceptable argumentative boundary desperate determined discipline jealous ought privilege rebellious stubborn unreliable

7 Listen

a 60 Listen to Mrs Hart and her son Danny. Tick (✓) the things that they talk about.

	Mrs Hart	Danny
1 a close relationship		
2 problems at school		
3 hard work		
4 help in the home		
5 getting angry		
6 privacy		
7 being untidy		
8 independence		

b 60 Listen again and complete the sentences.

Mrs Hart's point of view

1 When Danny was younger he was .... and ....
2 At home, he spends most of his time ....
3 He doesn't communicate with her unless ....
4 She went into his room because ....

Danny's point of view

5 He doesn't want to talk to his mother about ....
6 When she tries to check up on him, he usually ....
7 He lost his temper recently because she ....
8 She should understand that he ....

Portfolio 9

Write an opinion essay on the situation in Exercise 7.

- Describe the situation in your own words.
- Give your opinions on the people's behaviour.
- Suggest what they could do to improve the situation.

Include some of these expressions:

He/She should / shouldn't / ought to …
He/She should have / shouldn't have …
It's time he/she …
If he/she/they [did something], … would/wouldn't …
It would/might help if …

Quiz 9

a What do you remember about Unit 9? Answer all the questions you can and then check in the Student's Book.

1 What is the name of the TV show about troublesome teenagers in New Zealand?

....

2 Which adjective best describes the girl in picture A?

cheerful smart spoilt jealous

3 Circle the odd one out.

enthusiastic aggressive rebellious argumentative

4 Add prefixes to make opposite adjectives.

........respectful ....imaginative ....polite

5 There are mistakes in these sentences. Write the correct sentences.

Alex would better be not late for his appointment. He ought catch the 8:15 bus.

....

....

....

6 Choose the correct answer: A, B, C or D.

It's time you .... to control your emotions.

A learn **C** will learn

B learned **D** would learn

7 Use the words to make three expressions and write them with their definitions.

lose up out someone wind storm it

A to leave angrily ....

B to annoy someone ....

C to become angry ....

8 Look at picture B and circle the correct words.

His sister is getting on his *temper* / *nerves*, but he's trying to keep his *cool* / *peace*.

9 Complete the sentence with the correct form of the verbs.

I wish I .... (have) enough money to buy those jeans. I shouldn't .... (spend) so much last week.

10 Look at the last syllable in these words. Which have the /ə/ sound?

sensitive stubborn attraction equipment advantage

b 61 Listen and check your answers.

c Now look at your Student's Book and write three more quiz questions for Unit 9.

Question: ....
....
Answer: ....

Question: ....
....
Answer: ....

Question: ....
....
Answer: ....

10 Creating a buzz

1 Vocabulary

Advertising

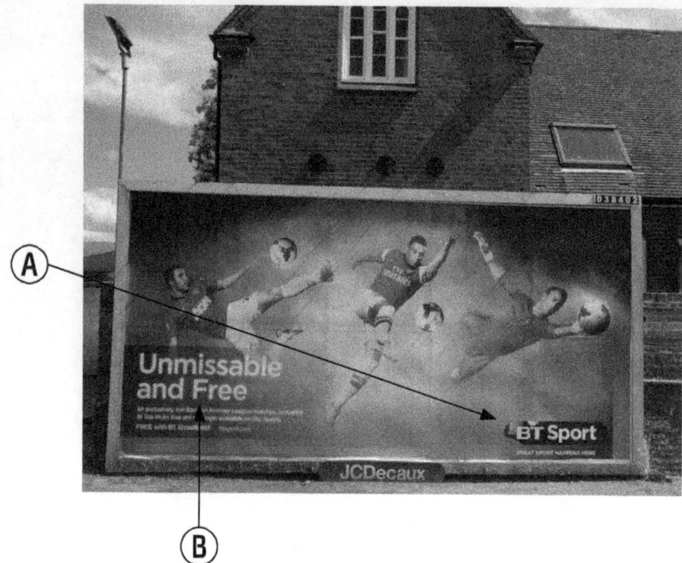

a Complete the crossword.

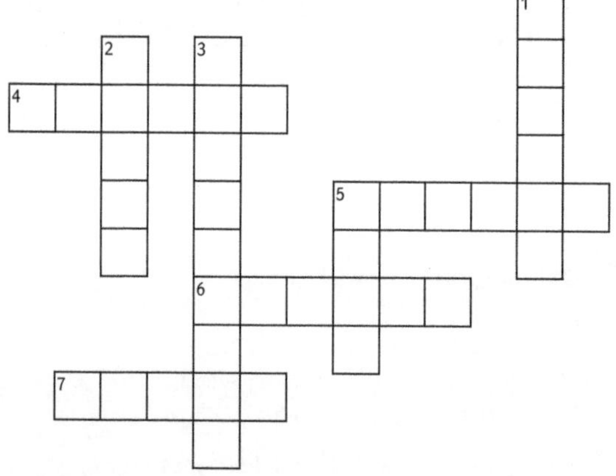

Across

4 In the photo, B is a ....
5 When companies .... a new product, they often spend a lot of money on advertising to grab people's attention.
6 In adverts for beauty products women are usually the .... customers.
7 Which .... of shampoo do you use?

Down

1 An advertising .... creates ideas for advertisements and then produces them.
2 When a .... ad appears on your computer screen, you have to click on a box to remove it.
3 They're planning to put a lot of adverts on tourist websites as part of their .... campaign.
5 In the photo, A is the company's ....

b Write examples of these things.

1 an unusual advertisement

....

2 an advertisement in which the target customers are teenagers

....

3 a top brand of footwear

....

4 an advertising slogan that gets on your nerves

....

5 a product that often appears in pop-ups

....

6 a new product that has been launched recently

....

2 Grammar

Grammar reference: page 98

Reporting verbs

a Circle the correct word.

1 He *warned / encouraged* us not to touch the plates because they were hot.
2 She *admitted / denied* stealing the camera and said she had bought it at Videoworld.
3 Customers are *explaining / complaining* that the game is difficult to install and causes their computers to crash.
4 The doctor has *advised / invited* me to do these exercises every day to make my knee stronger.
5 How can I *convince / order* you that I'm telling the truth?
6 Where have you been? We *offered / agreed* to meet at 7:30, didn't we?
7 I asked him to turn the music down, but he *refused / promised* to do it.
8 At the station they *mentioned / announced* that the train was running half an hour late due to the snow.

b 62 There are eight mistakes in this text. ~~Cross out~~ the wrong word(s) and write the correct word(s). Then listen and check. Sometimes there may be two correct answers.

An advert on the internet persuaded me getting this phone. They published reviews from customers who recommended people to buy it, and they also offered that it included free headphones and a battery. They promised delivering it within three days and it seemed like a good deal. Of course they didn't mention it to be a cheap, badly made product and I must admit that I didn't check it out. When I contacted the company and complained that the phone not to work properly, they refused that they take it back. Anyway, it's convinced me to not believe anything they say in adverts.

1 ....
2 ....
3 ....
4 ....
5 ....
6 ....
7 ....
8 ....

PHONETASTIC

Check it out!

For verbs with the infinitive, notice the difference between these negative forms.

I didn't promise to come. (= I didn't make this promise.)

I promised not to come. (= I said, 'I won't come.')

3 Vocabulary

Phrasal verbs with *come*

a Match the two parts of the sentences.

1 We're going to walk to the beach and come ☐
2 I've asked a few friends to come ☐
3 If you press this button, the menu will come ☐
4 Take advantage of opportunities that come ☐
5 How did you come up ☐
6 In the garage, she came ☐
7 I didn't know you'd met my cousin. How did that come ☐
8 When is the new Baz Luhrmann film coming ☐

A with that idea?
B up on your TV screen.
C across some old photos.
D back by bus.
E out?
F over on Sunday.
G about?
H along.

b Complete the sentences. Use the phrasal verbs with *come* from Exercise 3a.

1 I'm going to get the DVD as soon as it ....
2 Buses to the airport .... every 20 minutes.
3 I .... this information while I was surfing the net last night.
4 Paolo went out at four o'clock and he hasn't .... yet.
5 When I try to enter this site, an error message .... on the screen.
6 The side of our car has been damaged, but we don't know how that ....
7 I need to .... some new ideas for my website design.
8 I haven't seen you for a while. Why don't you .... next weekend?

Help yourself!

Separable and non-separable phrasal verbs

Look at these examples.

Separable

***Turn on** the light.* ***Turn** the light **on**.*

Non-separable

***I look after** my teeth.* (**not** ~~*look my teeth after*~~)

Are the sentences *correct* (✓) or *incorrect* (✗)?

1 **a** I put on my jacket. ☐
b I put my jacket on. ☐
2 **a** Children pick up languages easily. ☐
b Children pick languages up easily. ☐
3 **a** Where do you get on the train? ☐
b Where do you get the train on? ☐
4 **a** I'll pay back the money tomorrow. ☐
b I'll pay the money back tomorrow. ☐
5 **a** We checked into our hotel. ☐
b We checked our hotel into. ☐

Some dictionaries show the difference between separable and non-separable verbs. Check to see if your dictionary does this.

4 Read

a Read the two texts and choose the correct answers: A, B or C.

1 The first text is written for
  A teenagers.
  B advertising agencies.
  C companies with products to sell.

2 The second text is written by
  A a teenager.
  B a parent.
  C a market researcher.

The teen market can be difficult to target, but it presents a golden opportunity for any advertiser. Teens spend billions of dollars on goods and services. [1]........ And they are at a stage when they will soon begin to make big spending decisions on their own. [2]........ If you are successful, you can persuade these customers to form a life-long attachment to your brand.

Why choose us?

- We have over ten years' experience in managing teen marketing campaigns in the areas of entertainment, sport, beauty and technology.
- [3]........ We conduct up-to-date research into the latest trends in teens' use of different media, both online and offline.
- Our knowledge and experience will allow us to come up with all the solutions for the placement of your product. [4]........
- We will use the best combination of TV, online and print media to create an effective advertising campaign for the profitable teenage market.

Teenagers are always being warned about the effects of advertising, but lots of us are smarter about adverts than people think. We've grown up surrounded by ads. [5]........

For example, to me, billboards are just background. [6]........ I use software to block pop-ups on websites and on my phone. When I watch streamed video, I usually cut out the ads so as not to interrupt the programme. When I'm watching normal TV and the ads come on, I often flick over to other channels or I use the ad break to go and do something else.

It's true that I do like looking at some adverts. [7]........ But that doesn't mean I'm going to run out and buy the product they're advertising. Maybe this is just me, but I think lots of people of my age are similar. We don't buy something just because it's a trendy brand with clever advertising. We have to be convinced that the quality is good. [8]........ When we can see that an ad is fake or it's trying to make us buy something that's rubbish, we switch off.

b Find the correct places in the texts for the sentences.

A They can provide useful information, and also they can be fun.
B Patterns of behaviour are changing all the time.
C Your ideas need to be on-target to reach this valuable market.
D Most of the time I ignore them.
E They influence their parents' decisions about what to buy.
F This will save you time and money.
G Most kids value honesty and they aren't fools.
H We know what they're trying to do and we don't let them control us.

c What is the aim in the first text? Do you agree with the opinions in the second text? Prepare to talk about this in your next lesson.

5 Grammar Grammar reference: page 94

Participle clauses

a Complete the sentences with the present participle or the perfect participle.

Check it out!

When the participle clause comes first, it must have the same subject as the main clause.

Looking *at Sofia, ~~she was~~ upset.*
Looking *at Sofia,* ***we could see*** *she was upset.*

Having called *Don, ~~he wasn't~~ at home.*
Having called *Don,* ***I knew*** *he wasn't at home.*

1 .... (look) from the top window, you get a lovely view of the sea.
2 .... (leave) home at half past seven, I was at the station before eight o'clock.
3 Before .... (go) out, Sally washed her hair and changed her clothes.
4 .... (take off) late, the plane didn't arrive until after midnight.
5 Michael earned some extra money by .... (work) on Saturdays.
6 She speaks English fluently, ... (live) in Canada until she was fourteen.

b Complete the sentences with the present participle or the past participle.

Check it out!

Remember that the difference between the two participles is that the present participle is active while the past participle is passive.

1 The guy .... (stand) there is my brother.
2 I prefer wearing shoes .... (make) of leather.
3 She's going to buy one of those vacuum cleaners .... (advertise) on TV.
4 The pollution was caused by chemicals .... (come) from the factory
5 We got a phone call from our neighbour .... (complain) about the noise.
6 This product, ... (recommend) by doctors, is available in all good supermarkets.

c Complete the sentences with participle clauses.

1 The girl .... (wear / the striped jumper) is the team captain. .... (break / her wrist), she can't play in the match today.

2 .... (while / travel / in Brazil), we tried to communicate in Portuguese. That's the main language .... (speak / there).

3 .... (steal / the jewellery), they got into a black car .... (park / outside).

6 Pronunciation

Pitch in signalling words

a 63 **Listen and tick (✓) the sentences that start at a high pitch.**

1 Right, if everyone's ready, let's make a start. ☐
2 Unfortunately, we don't yet know the answer to that question. ☐
3 Now, the next topic I want to discuss is this. ☐
4 Therefore it's hard for people to find jobs. ☐
5 Finally, I'd like to talk about public transport. ☐

b 64 **People speaking in advertisements often use high pitch for certain words to express enthusiasm. Listen and tick (✓) the sentences that sound like advertisements.**

1 Wow! It really works. ☐
2 This is the best car on the market. ☐
3 So start your morning with a burst of energy. ☐
4 It has more cleaning power than any other product. ☐
5 Martin's are having a huge winter sale. ☐
6 But hurry. The sale must end on Saturday. ☐

c 65 **We make sudden rises in pitch to express strong feelings or to give special emphasis to a word. Listen and underline the words that have high pitch. Then listen again and repeat.**

1 Oh no! I think I've lost my passport!
2 Hey! I think that's a brilliant idea.
3 No, I asked for white coffee, not black.
4 That's my jacket, not yours, so give it to me!

66 Practise saying these words

advertising announce commercial
convince distribute launch persuade
promote publicity slogan target warn

7 Listen

a 67 **Listen to four people talking about advertisements. Match each speaker with a type of ad (1–6) and a product (A–F).**

1 TV ad **2** pop-up ad **3** magazine ad
4 poster **5** flyer **6** billboard

A food **B** a medical product **C** a gym
D a printer **E** a film **F** a perfume

Craig ☐ ☐ Tara ☐ ☐
Amy ☐ ☐ Josh ☐ ☐

b 67 **Listen again. Complete the sentences.**

Craig

1 The advert shows a .... out of someone's mouth.
2 The advert has persuaded Craig to ....

Tara

3 The ad promises ....
4 Everyone complains ....

Amy

5 There's a fat middle-aged man .... of the sign.
6 Amy thinks the advert is .... and ....

Josh

7 The target customers are ....
8 Having .... , the woman flies round the room.

Write an essay about an advertisement of your choice with young people as the target customers.

Paragraph 1

- What type of advert is it (e.g. billboard, TV ad, magazine ad, pop-up ad)?
- What is it advertising?
- Where / When / How often is it seen?

Paragraph 2

- What is shown in the advert?
- How do they aim to attract their target customers?

Paragraph 3

- How effective is it and why? Give your opinion.

Quiz 10

a What do you remember about Unit 10? Answer all the questions you can and then check in the Student's Book.

A

B

C O S U A L H G N O

1 **Choose two words to describe what is shown in picture A.**

buzz flash brand

agency customers mob

....

2 **What is the word for a type of advert that comes up on your screen when you are looking at a web page?**

....

3 **Find three advertising words in the puzzle in B to complete this sentence. Each word contains the letter L.**

Before they .... their new product, they need to design a .... and think of a good .... that people will remember.

4 **Match the verbs with their opposites.**

1 refuse	**A** warn
2 encourage	**B** deny
3 admit	**C** agree

5 **Complete the sentence with the correct form of the verbs.**

He recommended .... (take) the 9:30 train and offered .... (drive) me to the station.

6 **Read the sentence. Are the statements *right* (✓) or *wrong* (✗)?**

Coming downstairs, we heard the sound of voices.

A We were on the stairs when we heard voices. ☐

B We heard voices after we had come down. ☐

C People were talking as they came downstairs. ☐

7 **There are two mistakes in this sentence. ~~Cross out~~ the wrong words and write the correct ones.**

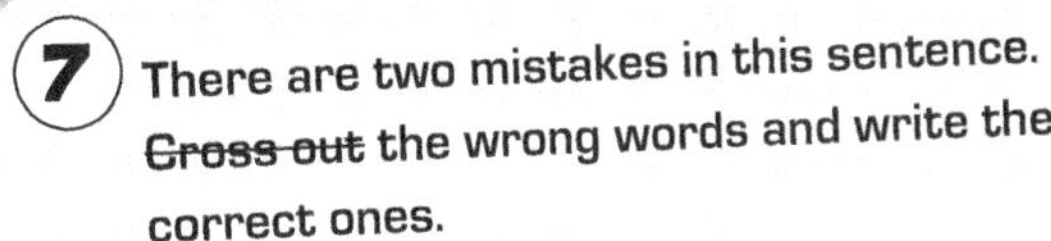

Hearing the band playing at the festival, Maria downloaded all the songs recording at their last concert.

....

8 **Join the sentences using two participle clauses.**

I was waiting for the bus. I saw a motorbike. It was painted green.

While ....

....

9 **Choose the correct answer: A, B or C.**

If you **come across** something, you

A search for something until you find it.

B find something that you weren't looking for.

C find something that you don't like.

10 **Circle the correct words.**

A big change came *up* / *across* / *about* when films with sound started to come *back* / *out* / *over* in the 1920s.

b 🔊 68 Listen and check your answers.

c Now look at your Student's Book and write three more quiz questions for Unit 10.

Question: ....
....
Answer: ....

Question: ....
....
Answer: ....

Question: ....
....
Answer: ....

11 Just the job

1 Vocabulary

Compound adjectives

a One word is wrong in each sentence. ~~Cross out~~ the wrong word and write the correct one.

1 Australia and New Zealand are English-spoken countries. ....
2 This bus company is privately own. ....
3 I can't read that sign without my glasses. I'm part-sighted. ....
4 They're having a two-weeks holiday in Switzerland. ....
5 Eduardo made a last-time decision to come with us. ....

b Complete the dialogue with compound adjectives.

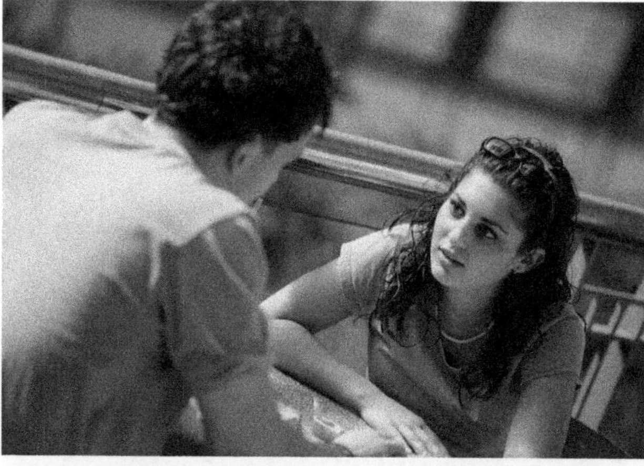

Greg: Cathy's got a good job with a cosmetics company. She's really happy there.
Alice: Oh, good. Is it a [1]p.............-t............. job?
Greg: Yes, she only works there from Monday to Wednesday. A [2]t.............-d............. week is ideal for her. She didn't want a [3]f.............-t............. job because she's still studying at college.
Alice: What about the pay?
Greg: Well, she isn't very [4]h............. p............. . But she can buy the cosmetics for a low price, which is good because they're [5]t.............-q............................ products. A lot of [6]w.............-f............................ celebrities use them, apparently.
Alice: Well, that's great. I'm glad she's found something that suits her.

Help yourself!

Compound adjectives with parts of the body

A *hot-headed* person is someone who loses their temper easily. A *cold-hearted* person is unkind and has no sympathy for other people.

Try to guess the compound adjectives for these meanings. Use a word from each box. Then check in your dictionary.

pig blue absent warm thick

skinned eyed hearted headed minded

1 kind and generous ....
2 stubborn ....
3 insensitive ....
4 having blue eyes ....
5 forgetful ....

2 Grammar Grammar reference: page 96

Modals of deduction and possibility review

Check it out!

For negatives, we can use *might/may not (have)*, but not *must not (have)*.

*They **might not** have arrived yet.*
*They **can't** have arrived yet.* (**not** ~~*must not have*~~)

a Match the two parts of the sentences.

1 That's a crazy story! You
2 I'm not sure who painted that picture, but it
3 They left work an hour ago. They
4 Marta isn't answering her phone. She
5 My iPod isn't here. I think someone
6 I lent him £30 this morning. He

A may have stolen it.
B can't have spent it already!
C might be by Rembrandt.
D can't be serious!
E must have switched it off.
F must get here soon.

b 69 Choose the correct answer: A, B or C. Then listen and check.

James: I'm trying to check in for my flight to Madrid, but their website is refusing to recognise my booking number.
Teresa: That's strange. Are you sure you've used the right number? You could [1]........ a mistake when you were typing it in.
James: No, look. This is the number and I've tried it three times. That [2]........ be the problem.
Teresa: Well, there [3]........ a problem with their computer system. There's no other explanation. I think you should leave it and try again in an hour. It [4]........ OK by then.

1 **A** make **B** made **C** have made
2 **A** can't **B** may not **C** mustn't
3 **A** can be **B** must be **C** must have been
4 **A** might be **B** must be **C** might have been

Grace: No, my purse definitely isn't here. It's gone!
Patrick: OK, now think. When did you last see it?
Grace: Well, I paid for my bus ticket, so I [5]........ it then. And when I got here my bag was closed, so the purse [6]........ dropped out.
Patrick: I guess you [7]........ it on the bus, though. How about ringing the bus company?
Grace: Yes, I suppose I could try that.
Patrick: If someone finds it, they [8]........ it to the driver, which means it will go to the Lost Property office at the bus station.

5 **A** might have **B** must have **C** must have had
6 **A** can't **B** can't have **C** mustn't have
7 **A** may leave **B** might leave **C** might have left
8 **A** might give **B** must give **C** might have given

c Use your own ideas to make replies with modal verbs.

1 A: I don't think this machine is working properly.
B: ....
....

2 A: Kim and Leah aren't speaking to each other for some reason.
B: ....
....

3 A: All the doors were locked, so how did the burglars get in?
B: ....
....

4 A: I expected to see Sam at the gym yesterday, but he wasn't there.
B: ....
....

3 Vocabulary

Job collocations

a Write the job collocations. Use words from both boxes.

be be have go apply write

for a job on strike your CV fired an interview promoted

1 to make a record of your qualifications and work experience

....

2 to ask formally for a job (usually by writing a letter/email or filling in a form)

....

3 to talk and answer questions so employers can decide if they want to give you a job

....

4 to be given a higher position at work

....

5 to be ordered to leave a job

....

6 to stop working to protest against something you think is unfair

....

b Complete the crossword.

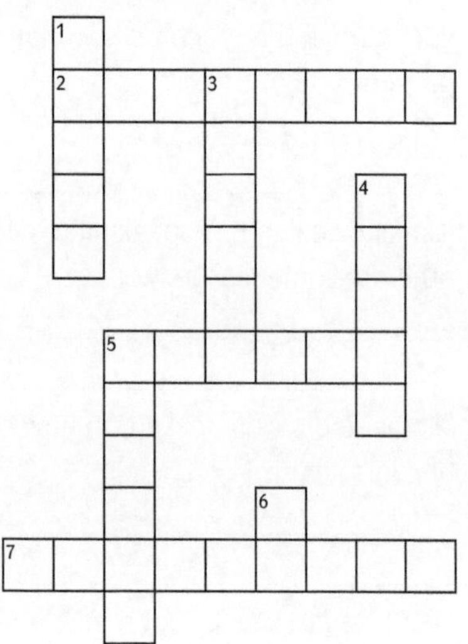

Across

2 Stefan started off as a shop assistant, but he's been .... He's a junior sales manager now.

5 The workers are going on .... to protest against their new contracts.

7 Yesterday Carla had an .... for a job at the museum. She was nervous, but she thinks she answered the questions quite well.

Down

1 I'm going to .... for a job that was advertised in the newspaper.

3 Jessica is a part-time .... of staff.

4 Ben was .... from his job because he didn't work hard and often arrived late.

5 Mum has to work .... in her job at the hospital. Sometimes she works from midnight to 8:00 a.m.

6 When you write your .... , don't forget to include all your previous work experience.

4 Listen

a 70 Listen to Louise talking to a careers adviser. Tick (✓) the photo that shows the job they are discussing.

A 
Flight attendant

B 
Tour guide

C 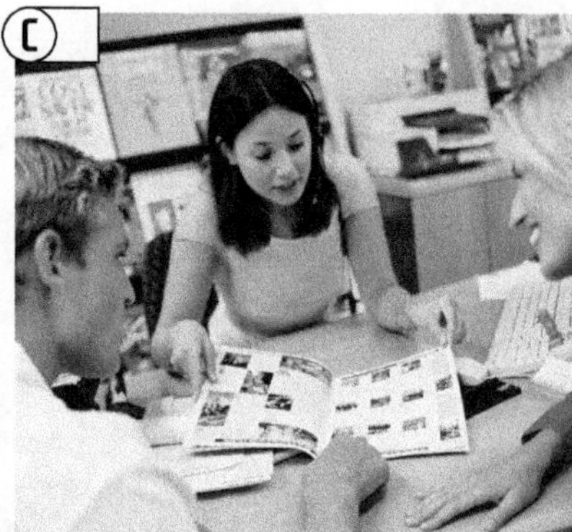
Travel agent

b 70 Listen again and tick (✓) the correct answers.

1 Do you need to research information in this job?
Yes ☐ No ☐

2 What sort of person should you be?

hard-working	☐	sympathetic	☐
confident	☐	reliable	☐
sociable	☐	ambitious	☐
creative	☐		

3 Is the job highly paid?
Yes ☐ No ☐

4 Is it easy to get promoted?
Yes ☐ No ☐

5 Do you need a university degree?
Yes ☐ No ☐

c 70 Listen again and complete the information.

Job conditions

- Deal with groups of up to [1]........................ people
- Free [2]........................ , ... and ....
- Sometimes a [3]........................-hour working day

Qualifications

- Basic training course: [4]........................ weeks
- In-depth course (part time): [5]........................ or .... months

d Would you like to have this job? Do you think you might be good at it? Prepare to talk about this in your next lesson.

5 Grammar Grammar reference: page 96

Question tag review

Check it out!

Don't forget this negative form with *I* + *be*:

I'm in your team, ***aren't I?*** (**not** ~~*am not I?*~~)

a Tick (✓) the sentence if the question tag is correct. If there is a mistake, ~~cross out~~ the wrong word in the question tag and write the correct word.

1 You're looking for a job, aren't you?

....

2 She isn't a member of staff, isn't she?

....

3 Your brothers work full time, don't they?

....

4 Mike won't earn much money in that job, would he?

....

5 The workers haven't gone on strike, did they?

....

6 You'd prefer to have a part-time job, don't you?

....

7 Sofia had an interview yesterday, hadn't she?

....

8 Show me your CV, will you?

....

b Complete the sentences with question tags.

1 Matt was doing a photography course at college last year, ... ?

2 You didn't enjoy that movie very much, ... ?

3 This isn't a car park. People shouldn't park their cars here, ... ?

4 The information about the course will be on the database, ... ?

5 Natalie's started taking singing lessons, ... ?

6 We can't take dictionaries into the exam room, ... ?

7 I'm in a difficult situation, ... ?

8 This food tastes great, ... ?

6 Pronunciation

Intonation in question tags

a 71 You will hear the sentences read twice, with rising and falling intonation. Listen and write 1 and 2 to show the order of the sentences.

	↗	↘
1 He's arriving on Tuesday, isn't he?	☐	☐
2 That phone call wasn't for me, was it?	☐	☐
3 Jane won't be here before six, will she?	☐	☐
4 I didn't hurt you, did I?	☐	☐
5 We can get a pizza here, can't we?	☐	☐
6 They've met each other before, haven't they?	☐	☐

b 72 Listen to the question tags. Draw arrows to show if the intonation is rising (↗) to check information or falling (↘) to ask for agreement. Then listen again and repeat.

1 They speak Spanish in Peru, **don't they?**

2 The exam wasn't very difficult, **was it?**

3 They'd like to go to the party, **wouldn't they?**

4 We're going in the wrong direction, **aren't we?**

5 You've met my parents, **haven't you?**

6 The storm caused a lot of damage, **didn't it?**

c 73 Would you expect rising or falling intonation in these question tags? Draw arrows: ↗ or ↘. Then listen, check and repeat.

1 It's cold this morning, **isn't it?**

2 You haven't seen my glasses anywhere, **have you?**

3 Wow! She looks great in that dress, **doesn't she?**

4 We'd better go. We don't want to be late, **do we?**

5 I haven't seen Jack lately. He isn't ill, **is he?**

6 I think they've gone to the beach, **haven't they?**

74 Practise saying these words

apply application candidate colleague employer junior kind-hearted lawyer qualification technique unpredictable well-behaved

7 Read

a Read the article. What is David Bloomfield's job?

....

The professional life of 22-year-old David Bloomfield takes many shapes. You might see him as a bad-tempered businessman, a money-hungry nephew, a suspicious neighbour or a jealous husband. Sometimes he may be a murder victim – or he may be a cold-hearted killer. David is a member of an acting company called Nightshade, who create and perform 'interactive murder mysteries'.

Although these events can be held in someone's home, they usually take place in a hotel, where guests come for an evening or a weekend. Having planned out a story in which at least one character will be killed, the actors play the main parts themselves. There is no stage – the audience is part of the scene as the action unfolds. Members of the audience share meals and conversations with the characters, they can ask questions and they listen for clues. At the end, like Poirot or Miss Marple, they have to solve the mystery and work out who the killer is.

David has been working with Nightshade for two years. At school he studied drama and he had leading roles in school theatre productions. But he might never have thought of this particular job if he hadn't had a stroke of luck. 'It happened by chance,' he explains. 'I was working at weekends as a waiter at the Grange Hotel where the company performs regularly. I'd watched their performances and I knew how the event worked. So when one of the actors became ill, I volunteered to take his part. It was a last-minute decision and they were taking a big risk with me, but I must have done quite well, because they invited me to stay with them for the rest of the season. And I'm still with them now.'

David is enthusiastic about his work. 'Mixing with the audience makes it a real challenge,' he says. 'Every event is different. You can't just rely on a script like most actors and you never know quite what to expect. You have to be creative and quick-thinking to create a convincing character while keeping the mystery alive. I love all that. It must be great to work in films or on a TV mystery series like *Poirot*, but I know I'd miss the buzz you get from interacting with a live audience.'

b Choose the correct answer: A, B or C.

1 In his job David has to
- **A** act as a businessman. ☐
- **B** play the part of a killer. ☐
- **C** perform in different roles. ☐

2 Interactive murder mysteries
- **A** may not take place in a hotel. ☐
- **B** are always performed at night. ☐
- **C** might tell a story about a crime. ☐

3 The people in the audience
- **A** are given roles to play. ☐
- **B** are involved in the action. ☐
- **C** can talk to the actors on stage. ☐

4 When David started work with the Nightshade company, he
- **A** had a part-time job. ☐
- **B** had experience as a professional actor. ☐
- **C** had been planning an acting career. ☐

5 He must have given a good performance because
- **A** he volunteered to replace someone. ☐
- **B** the company made a risky decision when they employed him. ☐
- **C** he was invited to keep acting with the company. ☐

6 David says his work is different from other acting jobs because
- **A** the scripts are unusual. ☐
- **B** interactive events are unpredictable. ☐
- **C** working in films or TV wouldn't be very enjoyable. ☐

Portfolio 11

Prepare questions to ask someone about their job. Then interview the person and write an article describing what he/she does. Include this information:

- when and how he/she got the job
- what qualifications and experience he/she had
- what the job involves
- whether he/she likes the job or not

Quiz 11

a What do you remember about Unit 11? Answer all the questions you can and then check in the Student's Book.

A

B

1 **How does the girl in picture A make a living?**

....

2 **Tick (✓) the true statements about the girl in picture A.**

A She's a 19-year-old girl. ☐

B She wants to be a world-famous writer. ☐

C She doesn't have a highly paid job. ☐

D She sometimes works a 16-hour day. ☐

3 **Use these words to make compound adjectives and complete the sentence.**

owned speaking part English time privately

He's an .... student who has a .... job with a .... bus company.

4 **Rewrite the sentence using the modal verb in brackets.**

It's possible that the information isn't on the database. (may)

....

....

5 **Choose the correct answer: A, B or C.**

You [1]........ a mistake. You [2]........ Fiona because she's away on holiday.

1 **A** might make **B** could make **C** must have made

2 **A** mustn't see **B** can't have seen **C** might not see

6 **Add vowels (*a*, *e*, *i*, *o*, *u*) to make words connected with jobs.**

ntrvw mmbr prmtd strk

A go on ....

B have an ....

C a .... of staff

D be ....

7 **Circle the correct words.**

I'm not going to *work* / *write* / *apply* for a factory job because I don't want to *work shifts* / *be fired* / *write my CV*.

8 **What is the job of the person in picture B?**

....

9 **Complete the sentence.**

You .... forget to call me, will you?

10 **Complete the dialogue with question tags.**

A: Peter enjoys his job, ...?

B: Yes, but it isn't well paid, ...?

b 75 Listen and check your answers.

c Now look at your Student's Book and write three more quiz questions for Unit 11.

Question: ....

....

Answer: ....

Question: ....

....

Answer: ....

Question: ....

....

Answer: ....

12 Changing times

1 Vocabulary

Expressions with *time*

a Read each sentence and then decide if the statement below is *right* (✓) or *wrong* (✗).

1 *Most of the time I wear casual clothes.*
I don't normally wear casual clothes. ☐

2 *They visit us from time to time.*
We get frequent and regular visits from them. ☐

3 *Why do you play that song all the time?*
Why do you keep playing that song? ☐

4 *He's one of the best footballers of all time.*
He's one of the best footballers who have ever lived. ☐

5 *José and Lisa were doing their homework at the same time.*
José and Lisa both had the same homework to do. ☐

b 76 Circle the correct words. Then listen and check.

My brother Ned met Sophie Gray when they were both 20 and they went out together [1]*at the same time / for a short time*. It was a very intense relationship and they even talked about getting married, but it would have been the biggest disaster [2]*of all time / all the time* if they'd done that. They loved each other, but [3]*from time to time / at the same time* they disagreed about everything and they used to argue [4]*for a short time / all the time*. They broke up about a year ago, although they still see each other [5]*of all time / from time to time*. Ned hasn't had another girlfriend since then and I know he still misses Sophie. But [6]*most of the time / all the time* he's quite happy and cheerful and I'm sure he knows they made the right decision.

Check it out!

The expression *all the time* can mean 'always, without stopping'.

The Earth is turning on its axis ***all the time****.*

However, it is more commonly used, especially in spoken English, to mean 'extremely often'.

I love that song! I play it ***all the time****.*

Why does he get so angry ***all the time****?*

2 Grammar

Grammar reference: page 98

Reported speech review

a Complete the reported sentences.

1 Eva: 'I'm watching TV.'
Eva said that .... TV.

2 Luke: 'Dad bought a new laptop.'
Luke said that .... father .... a new laptop.

3 Emma: 'My pizza isn't hot enough.'
Emma complained that .... pizza .... hot enough.

4 Sam: 'I'll come at seven o'clock.'
Sam promised that .... at seven o'clock.

5 Julia: 'I haven't met your parents.'
Julia said that .... parents.

6 Robbie: 'I can install the program for you.'
Robbie told us that .... the program for ....

Check it out!

Remember that when reporting someone's words, we sometimes have to change pronouns and possessive adjectives.

Kate: 'I'll call you later.'

Kate said ***she*** *would call* ***me*** *later.*

Ben: 'Have you seen my keys?'

Ben asked if ***we*** *had seen* ***his*** *keys.*

b Choose the correct answer: A, B or C.

1 'When is the new game coming out?'
Amir asked when the new game .... out.
A came **B** had come **C** was coming

2 'Do you like Ugg Boots?'
Lucy asked Alan .... Ugg Boots.
A does he like **B** did he like
C whether he liked

3 'Why is the film so popular?'
Bryan wanted to know why .... so popular.
A was the film **B** the film was
C the film had been

4 'Have you found your bracelet?'
Ella asked me .... found my bracelet.
A if I had **B** had I **C** whether I

5 'How long will I have to wait?'
Greg asked how long .... have to wait.
A he would **B** would he **C** did he

6 'Did everyone enjoy the party?'
Suzie asked if everyone .... the party.
A would enjoy **B** had enjoyed
C was enjoying

c Read the dialogue and complete the text using reported speech.

Mia:	[1]What do you think of my jacket?
Ryan:	Hey, [2]it looks great. [3]I haven't seen anything like it before.
Martina:	[4]Where did you buy it?
Mia:	I didn't buy it – [5]I made it myself.
Martina:	Cool! [6]Can I try it on?
Mia:	Yeah, sure. But [7]it'll probably be a bit too big for you.
Ryan:	Watch out, Mia. When Martina puts on that jacket, [8]she won't want to give it back.

Mia asked Ryan and Martina [1] ....
....

Ryan replied that [2] .... and said that [3] ....
.... before.

Martina asked Mia [4] ....
.... and Mia explained that [5] ....
....

Then Martina asked [6] ....
....

Mia said yes, but told Martina that [7] ....
....

Ryan warned Mia that when Martina put on the jacket, [8] ....
....

3 Listen

a 77 Listen to Natalie, Mark and Jessica talking about three different fads. Match the names with the correct photos.

1 Beanie Baby ☐ 2 Yo-yo ☐
3 Space Invaders ☐

A

B

C

D

E

b 77 Listen again and complete the sentences.

Natalie

1 Natalie said that Beanie Babies ....
.... in the 1990s.

2 She told us that her uncle ....
.... in his cupboard.

3 She asked whether they ....
....

Mark

4 Mark told us that the ancient Greek cup ....
.... years old.

5 He said that his friend George ....
.... of yo-yos.

6 He added that George ....
an international competition.

Jessica

7 Jessica asked if anyone still ....
....

8 She explained that the monsters ....
.... all the time.

9 She also mentioned that from time to time
....

4 Grammar Grammar reference: page 100

Relative clause review

a Underline the relative clauses and add commas if necessary. Write D (defining relative clause) or N (non-defining relative clause).

1 *Ketchup* comes from a Chinese word which means tomato sauce. ....
2 People who talk during a film are really annoying. ....
3 That's my friend Elena whose father is a TV journalist. ....
4 Polish is the language that we normally speak at home. ....
5 The restaurant where John works has been bought by new owners. ....
6 Leo and Cathy who live in Sweden are coming to stay with us next month. ....
7 Mrs Fields whose flat is next door to ours teaches English at Justin's school. ....
8 The hotel where we'll be staying is very close to the beach. ....

b Complete the relative clauses with relative pronouns. Sometimes there may be two correct answers. Add commas if necessary.

Check it out!

Remember that *whose* is always followed by a noun, and *where* is always followed by a noun or pronoun.

1 Lots of tourists visit the house .... Shakespeare was born.
2 Our neighbour .... hardly ever buys a lottery ticket won £14,000 last Saturday.
3 We were disappointed by the second film .... wasn't as good as the first one.
4 I feel so sorry for all the people .... homes were destroyed by the hurricane.
5 Is there anyone .... can give me some advice about this problem?
6 Isabel .... mother tongue is Spanish speaks English fluently.
7 You need to get on the train .... goes to Brighton.
8 We walked to the café in Carlton Street .... we stopped for a milkshake.

c Join the two sentences using a relative clause.

A: [1]Can you see the building? It's going up over there.
B: Yes, what is it?
A: [2]That's the stadium. The athletics championships will be held there.

1 Can you see ....
....
2 ....
....

A: [3]Do you know the man? He's talking to your mother.
B: [4]He's Mr Lao. His family runs the Red Lantern restaurant.
A: Oh, we went there last Saturday. [5]I tried one of their duck dishes. It was delicious.

3 ....
....
4 ....
....
5 ....
....

Check it out!

The pronouns *who*, *which* and *that* can sometimes be left out, but only

- in a defining relative clause.
- when the pronoun is the object of the clause, not the subject.

Tom is the person ***you should talk to****.*
(= who/that you should talk to)

I like the shirt ***she was wearing last night****.*
(= that/which she was wearing)

5 Vocabulary

Loan words in English

a Look at the table: 6 is A, 13 is T and 15 is E. Write all these letters in the puzzle. Then complete the loan words and write the letters in the table.

1	2	3	4	5	6	7	8	9	10
					A				

11	12	13	14	15	16	17	18	19	20
		T		E					

					1	2	3	4	1						16
	5				6			7							6
8	3	9	10	11	12	13		6				7			14
	4				6			9				2			14
	17				3		18	10	6	5	7	6	9	19	15
	11				1			15				19			13
	2				15			13				3			
	13							13							
	3						20	2	15	4	13	6			

b Add vowels (*a*, *e*, *i*, *o*, *u*) to make loan words and use them to complete the sentences.

bllt ssh ksk ktchp msqt spghtt

1 Do you want some .... on your hamburger?
2 You can buy drinks and sweets at the ....
3 She's a very talented .... dancer.
4 Don't scratch that .... bite.
5 My favourite Japanese food is ....
6 I'm cooking .... with tomato sauce.

c What are some loan words from English in your language?

....

....

....

6 Pronunciation

Pronouncing loan words in English

a 78 All the words in this list are loan words from other languages. Listen and practise saying them with their English pronunciation.

café opera hamburger curry
algebra karaoke theory restaurant
shampoo rucksack studio omelette

b 79 You will hear these place names twice. Write 1 if the English pronunciation comes first and 2 if it comes second.

Mexico ☐ Tokyo ☐ Brazil ☐
Berlin ☐ Portugal ☐ Paris ☐
Madrid ☐ Buenos Aires ☐

c 80 Some place names have been anglicised (given an English form). Tick (✓) the English version of these cities. Then listen, check and repeat.

1 Roma ☐ Rome ☐
2 Praha ☐ Prague ☐
3 Lisbon ☐ Lisboa ☐
4 Venice ☐ Venezia ☐
5 Sevilla ☐ Seville ☐
6 Moscow ☐ Moskva ☐
7 Napoli ☐ Naples ☐
8 Athens ☐ Athina ☐

81 Practise saying these words

awareness ketchup mixture native
naturally official preferable reject
standard switch theory variety

Help yourself!

English words with Latin roots

A lot of English words come from Latin. Try to think of at least one English word from each of these Latin verbs.

1 porto (= I carry)

....

2 scribo/scriptus (= I write / written)

....

3 video/visus (= I see / seen)

....

4 scio (= I know)

....

5 loco (= I put or place)

....

6 facio/factus (= I make or do / made or done)

....

7 Read

a Read the question and the replies in the language forum. What is the main topic in each reply? Match the names with the topics.

Paul ☐ Matthew ☐ Olivia ☐ **1** reading **2** speaking **3** listening

FrenchForum

We're interested in your experiences. What problems have you had in learning French and what tips do you have for others who are learning a foreign language?

Replies

paulconway

I've been studying French for six years and it's still quite difficult to understand native speakers, who often talk too quickly for me. One thing that I find useful is watching French films on DVD, which I enjoy doing. The English subtitles help me to pick up the French dialogue, but when it's a film that I've seen before, I already know more or less what people are saying so I don't use the subtitles. I find that the more you listen, the easier it gets. You really know you're getting somewhere when you just hear the words and don't have to translate all the time.

Matt999

Our teacher told us it was important to read as much as possible in French and I can see that's true. But you have to find things that interest you – otherwise it gets boring and you give up. I visit French-speaking music websites, where I can get information and follow discussions about the music that I like. I don't understand every word, but I find I can guess a lot without having to use a dictionary. I learn a lot this way, and it doesn't feel like work because I'm reading about things that are relevant to me.

olivia

I'm quite good at learning the grammar and vocabulary, so I do well in written exams, but speaking in French has always been a problem for me. I get nervous – I feel like an idiot because I know I'm making mistakes all the time. But I've been feeling better about this lately because of my friend Gérard, who lives in Toulouse. He's finally convinced me to just have a go and not to worry so much. It doesn't matter if you get things wrong – the main thing is to try to communicate. We talk on Skype, sometimes in English and sometimes in French, and Gérard helps me out if I get stuck. I get a real buzz when I say things in French and find that he can understand me.

b Complete the sentences with the correct names.

1 .... uses his/her interest in movies to help with the language.

2 .... is in touch with someone who lives in a different country.

3 .... says it is sometimes hard to follow what French people are saying.

4 .... has got more confidence recently.

5 .... often reads French online.

c Answer the questions.

1 According to Paul, why are native speakers hard to understand?

....

2 When does Paul switch off the subtitles for a French film?

....

3 What does Matt use to help improve his French?

....

4 In Matt's opinion, what sort of reading material should people look for?

....

5 Why does Olivia get good marks in French?

....

6 In her opinion, what is the most important thing to do when you're speaking a foreign language?

....

Portfolio 12

Write a comment for a similar website about learning English. Describe your own experience.

- How long have you been learning English?
- What are you good at?
- What do you find difficult?
- What tips can you give for other English learners?

Quiz 12

We're going to hanguear at the mol.

a What do you remember about Unit 12? Answer all the questions you can and then check in the Student's Book.

1 **Choose the correct answer: A, B or C.**

A fad is something that

A lots of people wear.

B becomes fashionable for a short time.

C is popular because it is inexpensive.

2 **Which famous sports person launched Livestrong bracelets?**

....

3 **Use the words in both boxes to make four *time* expressions.**

all the | most of | from time | at the

to time | time | same time | the time

....

....

4 **Complete the sentence with a *time* expression.**

Picasso was one of the greatest painters ....

5 **Complete the sentence in reported speech.**

Adam: 'I don't think it's going to rain.'

Adam said that ....

....

6 **Circle the correct words.**

Amy: 'Has Charlie spoken to you?'

Amy asked *if / that* Charlie *spoke / had spoken* to *her / me*.

7 **What is the 'language' in picture A?**

....

8 **Complete the sentence with the correct relative pronouns.**

Seaford, ... is on the south coast, is the town .... my father was born.

9 **Join the two sentences using a relative clause.**

Czech isn't a difficult language for Olga. Her mother tongue is Russian.

....

....

10 **Find four things which are loan words in picture B.**

s _ _ _ _ c _ _ _ _ _ _ _ _

p _ _ _ _ s _ _ _ _ _ _ _ _

b 82 Listen and check your answers.

c Now look at your Student's Book and write three more quiz questions for Unit 12.

Question: ....
....
Answer: ....

Question: ....
....
Answer: ....

Question: ....
....
Answer: ....

Grammar reference

1 Simple and continuous tense review

Present simple	Present continuous
Jane usually **sits** at the back of the bus. He **doesn't work** on Sundays. **Do** you often **go** to the cinema?	Jane **is sitting** in the garden at the moment. He **isn't working** today. Hi, Rosa. Where **are** you **going**?
Past simple	**Past continuous**
We **walked** into the room and **sat** down. He **didn't work** hard enough last term. **Did** you **go** to the gym yesterday?	At 1:00 yesterday we **were sitting** in the café. I couldn't call you because my phone **wasn't working**. I saw you in Park Street. **Were** you **going** to the gym?

- We use the present simple for permanent situations and regular or repeated actions in the present. We also use it to describe events in a book or film.
- We use the present continuous for actions that are in progress now. We also use it for future arrangements.
- We use the past simple for completed actions in the past. It is often used with past time expressions (*last month*, *two weeks ago*, etc.).
- We use the past continuous for actions that were in progress over a period of time in the past. It often describes what was happening at a certain time.
- We can use the past simple and past continuous together. The past continuous action is longer and started earlier. It was already in progress when the past simple action happened.
  *They **were having** dinner when I **arrived**.* *He **got** the injury while he **was playing** football.*
- We don't normally use the continuous form for these verbs:
  like love hate prefer want need know believe understand agree belong own mean

★ For more notes on future arrangements, see page 80.

★ For a list of irregular verbs, see page 102.

2 Perfect tense review

Present perfect simple	Present perfect continuous
I've stayed in this hotel before. They **haven't won** any matches yet. **Has** she **finished** her homework?	**I've been staying** here since last Friday. They **haven't been playing** well lately. **Has** she **been doing** her homework every day?

- The present perfect tenses always make a connection between the past and the present.
- We use the present perfect simple to talk about actions at some time in the past up to now.
  *Jill **has rung** me three times today.* (= from the start of the day up to now)
  ***Have** you ever **been** to Brazil?* (= at any time in your life up to now?)
- We use the present perfect simple for past actions that directly affect the present. They are often recent actions.
  *Someone **has stolen** my wallet!* (It isn't here now!) ***Has** he **arrived** yet?* (Is he here now?)
- We use the present perfect simple with *for* and *since* for actions that started in the past and are still happening now.
  ***I've known** Ali for five years.* (I still know him now.) *We**'ve been** here since 10:30.* (We're still here now.)
- We use the present perfect continuous for actions that have been in progress over a period of time up to now. The action may have finished recently or it may still be happening now.
  *Eva **has been talking** on the phone for over an hour.* *How long **have** you **been waiting** here?*

★ For irregular past participles, see page 102.

Grammar practice

1 Simple and continuous tense review

Complete the text with the correct form of the verbs.

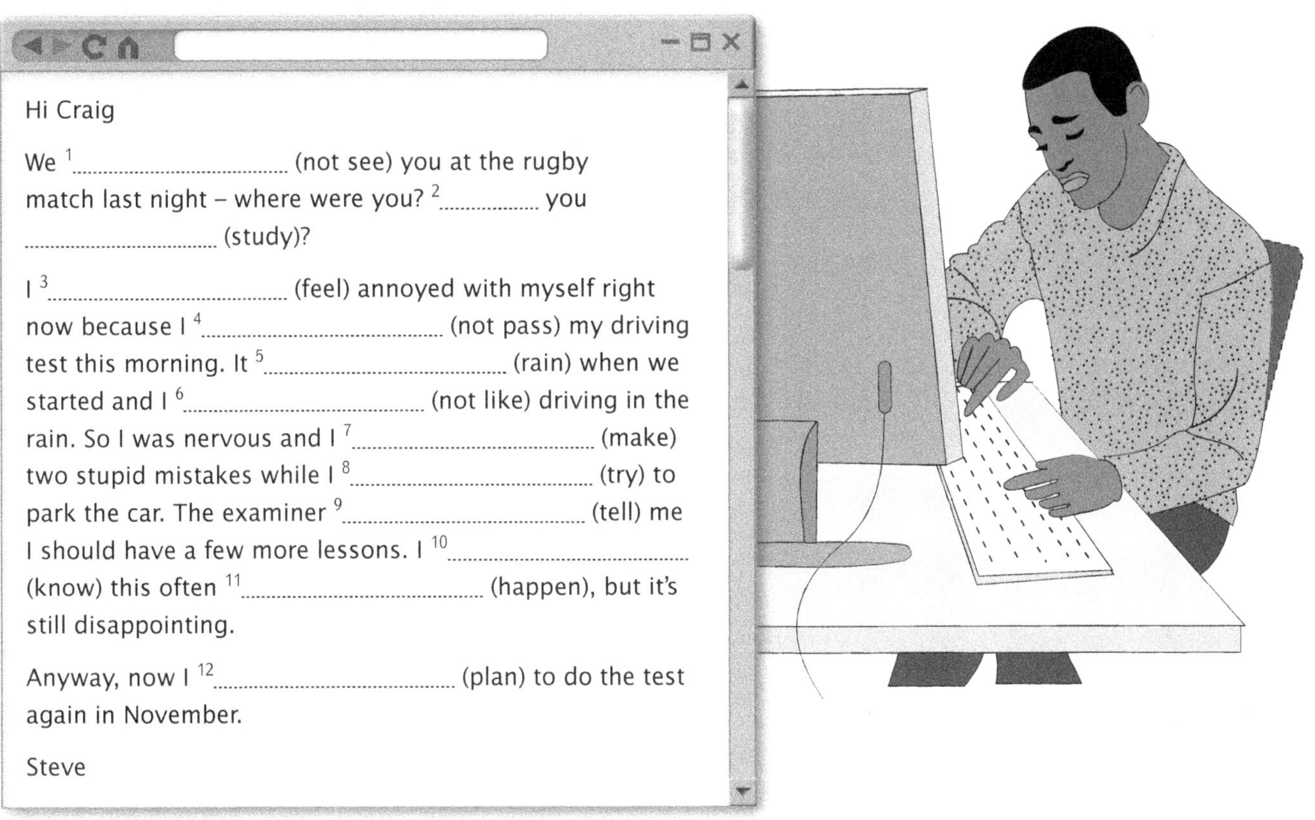

Hi Craig

We [1] .... (not see) you at the rugby match last night – where were you? [2] .... you .... (study)?

I [3] .... (feel) annoyed with myself right now because I [4] .... (not pass) my driving test this morning. It [5] .... (rain) when we started and I [6] .... (not like) driving in the rain. So I was nervous and I [7] .... (make) two stupid mistakes while I [8] .... (try) to park the car. The examiner [9] .... (tell) me I should have a few more lessons. I [10] .... (know) this often [11] .... (happen), but it's still disappointing.

Anyway, now I [12] .... (plan) to do the test again in November.

Steve

2 Perfect tense review

a Circle the correct verb.

1 You don't have to cook tonight. I've already ***made / been making*** a lasagne.
2 Daniel should go outside and get some exercise. He's ***sat / been sitting*** inside all day.
3 This weather is depressing! It's ***rained / been raining*** for three days now.
4 I haven't ***met / been meeting*** Pete's girlfriend. How long have they ***gone / been going*** out together?
5 Alice has ***lost / been losing*** her umbrella. Have you ***seen / been seeing*** it anywhere?

b Complete the sentences. Use the present perfect simple or the present perfect continuous.

1 Diego .... just .... (come) home. He .... (work) all day.
2 I'm glad you .... (decide) to go to bed early. You .... (not get) enough sleep lately.
3 Yasmin .... (plan) this trip for ages. .... she .... (book) her flight yet?
4 We .... (try) to find you! What .... you .... (do)?
5 My sister Lily .... (look) for a new job for the past few weeks, but she .... (not find) anything suitable yet.

3 Perfect tense review

Past perfect simple	Past perfect continuous
The match **had started** when we got there.	They**'d (had) been playing** for ten minutes.
I knew she **hadn't heard** what I'd said.	She **hadn't been listening**.
He got home at 1:00 a.m. Where **had** he **been**?	What **had** he **been doing**?

- The past perfect simple is used when we are already talking about a time in the past. We use it to describe a completed action that happened before that time.

  *By the time she got to the cinema, the film **had** already **begun**.*
  *We were amazed by Steve's voice. We **hadn't heard** him sing before.*

✱ For irregular past participles, see page 102.

- The form *had* + past participle is the same for all subjects.
- We use the past perfect continuous for an action that was in progress over a period of time before a later event happened. We are showing that the earlier action continued for some time.

  *I wasn't surprised when he lost his job. **I'd been expecting** it for a long time.*
  *Ella left Berlin last year. She**'d been living** there since 2008.*
  *He **hadn't been driving** for long when he got his driving licence.*
  *A: Tom and Anna broke up two weeks ago. B: How long **had** they **been going** out together?*

- The form *had* + *been* + past participle is the same for all subjects.

4 *used to*, *be used to* and *get used to*

used to + infinitive

*My sister **used to love** the Jonas Brothers when she was younger.*
*I **didn't use to watch** documentaries, but I find them interesting now.*
*What **did** people **use to wear** in the 1950s?*

✱ Don't confuse *used to* + infinitive with the verb *use*.
*I **used to have** a slower computer.*
*I **used** my computer to design this poster.*

- We use *used to / didn't use to* + infinitive for actions that happened normally or frequently in the past, but don't happen now.
- The form is the same for all subjects.

be used to and *get used to*

*Polar bears **are used to** a cold climate.*
*He hadn't travelled outside the UK before, so he **wasn't used to** driv**ing** on the right.*
*The noise might annoy you at first, but you'll soon **get used to** it.*
*The conditions in the factory were terrible. I couldn't **get used to** work**ing** there.*

- We use *be/get used to* to talk about someone's familiarity with a situation that seemed strange earlier.
- *Be used to something* means 'to be familiar and comfortable with something'.
- *Get used to something* means 'to become familiar and comfortable with something'. It is often used with *can* or *could*.
- *Be used to* and *get used to* are followed by a noun/pronoun or by the *-ing* form of a verb.

Grammar practice

3 Perfect tense review

a Match the sentences.

1 They were too tired to go out last night. ☐
2 My aunt and uncle left Edinburgh in 2009. ☐
3 I introduced Ben to our neighbours. ☐
4 Luke didn't seem very interested in the film. ☐
5 My parents were upset when Mr Wilson died. ☐
6 Hasan went upstairs to change his clothes. ☐
7 Nicholas felt better when he took up running. ☐
8 Dad couldn't read the menu without his glasses. ☐

A They'd known him for a long time.
B Had he already seen it?
C He hadn't been getting enough exercise.
D He'd been working at the garage all morning.
E They'd been training for the marathon.
F He'd forgotten to bring them.
G They hadn't met him before.
H They'd been living there for 15 years.

b Tick (✓) the sentence if it is correct. If there is a mistake, ~~cross out~~ the wrong word(s) and write the correct word(s).

1 I haven't studied French before I came to this school. ....
2 Cristina didn't realise she had been losing her purse until the next day. ....
3 We really loved our visit to Rome – we hadn't been there before. ....
4 She'd got headaches for some time, so she went to see the doctor yesterday. ....
5 Matt was starving – he hadn't eaten anything since breakfast time. ....
6 Before I'd begun taking guitar lessons, I'd already learnt to read music. ....

4 *used to*, *be used* to and *get used to*

Choose the correct answer: A, B or C.

A: You didn't grow up here, did you? Where did you [1]........ to live?
B: In a village called Hadstock, near Cambridge. It's a tiny place compared with London. We [2]........ have a house there.
A: So [3]........ used to city life now?
B: Yes, it's good now, but it was quite hard for all of us at first. We weren't [4]........ surrounded by people all the time and it was hard to [5]........ to the traffic. I [6]........ to sleep very well at night because of the noise. Now I don't notice it at all, and I feel quite comfortable here.

	A	B	C
1	use	be used	used
2	used to	were used to	got used to
3	do you	are you	did you get
4	use to be	used to be	used to being
5	use	be used	get used
6	didn't use	didn't used	wasn't used

Grammar reference

5 *will, going to* and present continuous

- We use *will* + infinitive to make predictions about the future. The verbs *think, suppose, believe, hope, expect* and adverbs like *maybe, perhaps, probably* are often used with *will* predictions.
  *I think you'**ll enjoy** this film.   It probably **won't rain** on Saturday.   Where **will** we **be** in ten years' time?*
- We also use *will* for decisions made at the time of speaking. The decision may be an offer or a promise.
  *I **won't go** out now. It's too cold outside.   Let's meet at the café. **I'll buy** you a coffee.*
- We use *going to* + infinitive for future plans and intentions.
  *Eva **is going to buy** a car.   I'**m going to work** harder next term.   What **are** you **going to wear** tomorrow?*
- We also use *going to* for predictions based on present evidence. It seems as though the future outcome has been decided already.
  *The temperature is rising. It'**s going to be** hot tomorrow.*
  *It's already five to eight. We **aren't going to get** there on time.*

✱ *Will* and *going to* predictions are similar and often both forms are correct.

- We use the present continuous to talk about future arrangements, often for the near future.
  *I'**m meeting** Marta at 6:30.   The trains **aren't running** tomorrow.   What time **is** the race **starting**?*
- Arrangements with the present continuous are often similar to plans with *going to* and both forms may be correct. However, for an intention with no definite arrangement, we can't use the present continuous.
  *I'**m meeting** / **going to meet** her at 6:30.   I'**m going to work** harder.* (**not** ~~*I'm working*~~)

6 Future continuous

- We use the future continuous for actions that will be in progress at a time in the future.
  *At 8:00 the ferry **will be crossing** the English Channel.   This time tomorrow I'**ll be doing** my Science exam.*
  *What **will** you **be doing** at midnight on New Year's Eve?*
- We also use the future continuous for things that we expect to happen or intend to do. Used like this, it has almost the same meaning as the present continuous for arrangements or *going to* for intentions.
  *My friends **will be arriving** soon.*   (= *My friends **are arriving** soon.*)
  *I **won't be staying** up late tonight.*   (= *I'**m not going to stay** up late tonight.*)
  *What time **will** you **be leaving**?*   (= *What time **are** you **going to leave**?*)

7 Future perfect and future perfect continuous

Future perfect simple	Future perfect continuous
He's leaving Paris on Sunday. He **will have spent** three days there.	He **will have been staying** there for three days.
At the end of May I still won't have my licence. I **won't have had** my driving test by then.	I **won't have been driving** for long enough.

- The future perfect tenses describe a future action in relation to a later time in the future.
- We use the future perfect simple to show that an action will be completed before a later time in the future.
  *In a couple of minutes' time we **will have downloaded** all the tracks on this album.*
  ***Will** she **have completed** her work by tomorrow?*
- We use the future perfect continuous to show that an action will be in progress up to a later time in the future. Often the action will still be happening at that later time.
  *At the end of November, they **will have been living** here for eight years.*

Grammar practice

5 *will, going to* and present continuous

Circle the correct words. If both answers are possible, choose the best one.

1 *Will we have / Are we having* better public transport in the future?
2 Here comes the rain! *We'll get / We're going to get* soaked.
3 Claudia *will go / is going* into town this afternoon. She's *looking / going to look* for some boots.
4 **A:** *I'll put / I'm going to put* up the decorations this weekend.
B: Right. *I'll give / I'm going to give* you a hand with that.
5 He probably *won't need /isn't needing* to take a taxi. His plane *won't leave / isn't leaving* until 11:45.
6 The concert *will start / is starting* in 20 minutes and we've only sold 50 tickets. *It will be / It's going to be* a disaster!
7 *I'm painting / I'm going to paint* my room soon. I hope *it'll look / it's going to look* good.
8 **A:** *We'll meet / We're meeting* at the theatre at 7:30. *Will you get / Are you getting* there in time?
B: Yes, don't worry. I promise *I won't be / I'm not going to be* late.

6 Future continuous

Complete the sentences with the future continuous form of the verbs.

stay do fly wait relax not sing

1 My last exam is on Friday. Next week I .... on the beach!
2 This time tomorrow they .... over Russia on their way to Japan.
3 We're in Germany now, but when you get this postcard we .... at the youth hostel in Vienna.
4 Meet me at the stadium, OK? I .... for you at the south gate.
5 We're all leaving school soon. What .... we .... in a year's time?
6 Unfortunately, Olivia's got flu so she .... with the band tomorrow night.

7 Future perfect and future perfect continuous

Complete the dialogues. Use the future perfect simple or the future perfect continuous.

A: This trip has been a nightmare. By the time we get there, we [1]........................ .... (sit) in this train for over four hours.
B: Yes, and Dad [2]........................ .... (wait) for us at the station since six o'clock.

A: I'll pick up the tickets at about 7:30. [3]............ you .... (leave) work by then?
B: Yes, I think I'll get to the cinema at about eight, but I [4].. (not have) time to change my clothes.

A: My grandmother is still working as a set designer, but she's going to retire in July next year.
B: How long [5]............ she .... (work) in the theatre?
A: She [6].. (be) there for almost 30 years!

A: The chicken won't be ready at 7:30. It [7]............ .... (not cook) for long enough.
B: That means we [8]............ .... (not finish) eating when Jack comes to pick me up.
A: No. I hope he won't mind waiting for a while.

Grammar reference

8 Infinitive and *-ing* review

Verb + verb

- With verbs for likes/dislikes, a following verb is usually in the *-ing* form.
  *Do you **like sailing**? She **hates being** late. I **enjoyed talking** to him.*
- Other verbs followed by verb + *-ing* include:
  admit avoid deny imagine keep miss practise recommend suggest
  *Why do you **keep arguing** with me? I **practise diving** at the pool.*
- Some verbs are followed by *to* + infinitive. Examples include:
  agree arrange choose decide expect forget hope learn
  need offer plan prepare pretend promise seem want
  *We **arranged to meet** at 3:30. I've **decided not to go** out tonight.*
- The verbs *start*, *prefer* and *continue* can be followed by either form.
  *He's **started writing / to write** his essay.*
  *The band **continued playing / to play** until midnight.*

✱ It is possible to use *like*, *love* and *hate* with *to* + infinitive.

*He **likes to get** up early.*

*I **love to hear** people laugh.*

Would like/love/hate is <u>always</u> used with *to* + infinitive.

***I'd like to go** swimming tomorrow.*

✱ Verbs can also be followed by *to* + infinitive when the meaning is 'in order to do something'.

*We ran **to catch** the bus.*

*She's working **to earn** money.*

Preposition + verb

- With prepositions, a following verb is always in the *-ing* form.
  *Liam is good **at painting**. I'm not very keen **on listening** to jazz. Have you ever thought **of doing** karate?*

be + adjective + verb

- After the verb *be*, some adjectives can be followed by *to* + infinitive. Examples include:
  amazed dangerous determined difficult easy hard lucky (im)possible ready safe surprised
  *She was **surprised to see** us. Are you nearly **ready to leave**? It isn't **difficult to use** a webcam.*

remember, *stop* and *try* with *-ing* and the infinitive

- The verbs *remember, stop* and *try* can be followed by either form, but the meaning changes.

*I **remember locking** the door.* (= I locked the door earlier and I can remember it now.)
*I **remembered to lock** the door.* (= I remembered that I had to lock the door and then I did it.)
*You should **try playing** chess.* (= you should try it as an experiment.)
*You should **try to play** chess.* (= you should make an effort to do it.)
*They **stopped talking** to us.* (= they no longer talked to us.)
*They **stopped to talk** to us.* (= they stopped something else in order to talk to us.)

9 *as*, *like* and *such as*

- We use *as* + noun to talk about someone's job or role, or the way something is used.
  *My sister works **as** a journalist. He knows a lot, but he's not very good **as** a teacher.*
  *She is regarded **as** one of our best writers. You can use your phone **as** a camera.*
- We use *as* + a full clause (with a subject and verb) to talk about actions that happen in a similar way. When speaking informally, we may use *like* instead of *as*.
  *I added some garlic, **as** you suggested. We were hanging out at the surf club **like** we usually do on Saturdays.*
- We use *like* + a noun/pronoun or a verb with *-ing* to mean 'similar to'.
  *Lucy looks **like** her mother. I admire people **like** you. Walking in Death Valley was **like** being on the moon.*
- We use *like* or *such as* + noun for giving examples.
  *She enjoys team sports **like / such as** basketball.*
  *They grow vegetables, **like / such as** peas and beans.*

Grammar practice

8 Infinitive and *-ing* review

a Complete the table with the verbs in the box.

choose want hate imagine decide recommend enjoy expect hope keep

Verb + *-ing*		Verb + *to* + infinitive	
1	4	6	9 ....
2	5	7	10 ....
3		8	

b Circle the correct words.

1 It was impossible ***getting / to get*** tickets for the concert.
2 Snowboarding is similar to ***ride / riding*** a skateboard.
3 Hana is responsible ***for preparing / to prepare*** all the salads at the café.
4 It isn't safe ***swimming / to swim*** near those rocks.
5 We were amazed ***seeing / to see*** Adam on TV last night.
6 They finally succeeded ***in repairing / to repair*** the machine.
7 It should be easy ***finishing / to finish*** this work tonight.
8 We're really looking forward ***to seeing / to see*** you tomorrow.

c Complete the dialogue with the correct form of the verbs.

A: I know I need [1]........................ (get) more exercise and I've decided [2]........................ (do) something about it. I'm just not sure what I want to do.

B: Have you thought about [3]........................ (take) up football or rugby? You could try [4]........................ (get) into one of the school teams.

A: No, I don't want [5]........................ (do) that. I'm not interested in [6]........................ (run) around after a ball. I remember [7]........................ (play) football when I was a kid and I really hated it. I never learned [8]........................ (kick) the ball properly and I kept [9]........................ (get) injured. I'd like [10]........................ (try) something different – rock climbing, maybe.

9 *as, like* and *such as*

Tick (✓) the sentence if it is correct. If there is a mistake, ~~cross it out~~ and write the correct word(s).

1 David got a job like an engineer in London.

....

2 Does your sister look such as you?

....

3 This film is now regarded like a classic.

....

4 Australia has some unusual animals, such as koalas.

....

5 He loves chocolate, such as most people do.

....

6 You're behaving as a fool!

....

7 We used the fallen tree as a bridge to get across the river.

....

8 They're expected to win the championship, as they did last year.

....

Grammar reference

10 Adverbs

- Adverbs are often formed from an adjective with an *-ly* ending.
  *quick > quick**ly***   *safe > safe**ly***   *professional > professional**ly***
  *happ**y** > happ**ily***   *bus**y** > bus**ily***
  *suit**able** > suit**ably***   *incred**ible** > incred**ibly***
  *bas**ic** > basic**ally***   *automat**ic** > automatic**ally***   (**but** *publ**ic** > publ**icly***)
- Some adverbs are irregular. The adverb form of *good* is *well*. The adverbs *fast*, *early*, *late* and *hard* have the same form as the adjective.
- Adverbs usually describe a verb, but they may also describe an adjective or another adverb.
  *The car was travelling **slowly**.*   *This is a **deliciously** sweet dessert.*   *They performed **extremely** well.*
- When the verb has an object, the most common word order is verb + object + adverb.
  *She speaks English **fluently**.*   *I want to finish my homework **quickly**.*

> ✱ However, frequency adverbs usually go before the verb.
> *We **often/usually** have lunch here.*

- The adverbs *absolutely*, *completely*, *totally* and *entirely* usually go before a verb or an adjective.
  *I **totally** agree with you.*   *They were **absolutely** exhausted.*
- Other emphatic adverbs, e.g. *really*, *extremely*, *incredibly*, usually go before an adjective or adverb.
  *It's going to be **really** cold tomorrow.*   *She works **incredibly** hard.*
- The following adverbs often go at the beginning of a sentence: *suddenly*, *finally*, *eventually*, *luckily*, *(un)fortunately*, *personally*.
  ***Suddenly** the door opened.*   ***Personally**, I thought the book was too long.*
- The comparative form is usually *more* + adverb. However, for irregular adverbs, the comparative has the same form as the comparative adjective.
  *Could you speak **more slowly**, please?*   *He dresses **more fashionably** than his friends.*
  *You need to try **harder**.*   *Trains go **faster** than buses.*   *I can swim a lot **better** than I used to.*

11 Making comparisons

- We use a comparative adjective or adverb + *than* to compare things. To show a small difference between them we can add *a bit*, *a little* or *slightly*. To show a large difference we can add *far*, *much*, *a lot* or *a great deal*.
  *Your hair is **a bit longer than** mine.*   *This printer works **much more reliably than** my old one.*
- We repeat comparatives with *and* to show that a certain quality keeps increasing over time.
  *This film is becoming **stranger and stranger** / **more and more confusing**.*
  *The team played **better and better** / **more and more confidently** as the match went on.*
- We use *the* + comparative … *the* + comparative to show that one situation depends on another.
  ***The faster** you run, **the more quickly** your heart beats.*
  ***The better** the design is, **the more attractive** your website will be.*

  With comparative adjectives, we can sometimes leave out the verb *be*.
  The better the design, the more attractive your website (will be).
- We use *as* + adjective/adverb + *as* to talk about things being alike or equal in some way.
  *Jess is **as tall as** her brother.*   *The weather isn't **as bad as** it was last week.*
  *I can't sing **as well as** you.*   *Please come **as quickly as** you can.*

Grammar practice

10 Adverbs

a Complete the table.

Adjective	Adverb
special	1 ....
2	terribly
3	easily
complete	4 ....
late	5 ....
accidental	6 ....

Adjective	Adverb
bad	7 ....
unlucky	8 ....
9	early
10	well
unbelievable	11 ....
basic	12 ....

b Rewrite the sentences, adding the adverb form of the adjectives in brackets.

1 Eduardo played the violin. (beautiful)

....

2 My computer is working now. (good)

....

3 Mum has to get up early. (incredible)

....

4 I think that idea is crazy! (personal, complete)

....

5 He was driving the car. (extreme, fast)

....

6 I love an exciting game of football. (absolute, real)

....

11 Making comparisons

a Match the two parts of the sentences.

1 Try to check your work ☐
2 You look a lot older ☐
3 Digital cameras are getting better and ☐
4 I wish these instructions were a bit ☐
5 The harder you try, the ☐
6 Your face is as red ☐

A easier to understand.
B as a tomato!
C more successful you'll be.
D than your brother.
E more carefully.
F better all the time.

b There is a mistake in each sentence. ~~Cross out~~ the wrong word(s) and write the correct word(s).

1 Mexico City is far larger then Santiago. ....
2 As she waited to go on stage, she became more and more nervously. ....
3 I'm practising the piano very more regularly now. ....
4 In my opinion, English isn't so difficult as Portuguese. ....
5 They arrived a bit more early than we were expecting. ....
6 The more talented the musicians are, the more better the music sounds. ....

12 Expressing contrast

- We use *although / even though / though* and *in spite of / despite* to make a contrast.
- *Although*, *even though* and *though* are followed by a full clause (with a subject and verb). The words have the same meaning, but we don't normally use *though* at the beginning of a sentence.
  *We're good friends, **although / even though / though** we often disagree.*
  ***Although / Even though** they scored three goals, they didn't win the match.*
- *In spite of* and *despite* are followed by a noun/pronoun or the *-ing* form of a verb.
  *We're good friends, **in spite of / despite** our disagreements.*
  ***In spite of / Despite** scoring three goals, they didn't win the match.*
- If we want to use a full clause after *in spite of / despite*, we add *the fact that*.
  *We're good friends, **in spite of / despite the fact that** we often disagree.*

13 Reflexive pronouns and *each other*

- Reflexive pronouns and *each other* come after a verb. They can be the direct or indirect object of the verb or they can follow a preposition.
- We use a reflexive pronoun when the person/thing we are referring to is also the subject of the verb.

Singular	I > **myself** you > **yourself** he > **himself** she > **herself** it > **itself**
Plural	we > **ourselves** you > **yourselves** they > **themselves**

✱ We can also use reflexive pronouns for emphasis.
*Did you make this cake **yourself**?*

*Angela hurt **herself** when she fell. We've bought **ourselves** a new TV. He walked home by **himself**.*

- We use *each other* for a mutual action, when each person in a pair or group does something to the other(s). The subject is always plural.
  *We've known **each other** for ages. They gave **each other** presents. People should be kind to **each other**.*

14 Expressions of purpose, reason and result

Purpose	Reason	Result
for + noun or *-ing* *to / in order to / so as to* + infinitive *so that* + subject + verb	*because* + subject + verb *because of / due to / as a result of* + noun or *-ing*	*so* + subject + verb *therefore* + subject + verb

- We use *for*, *to / in order to / so as to* and *so that* to talk about someone's aim or goal when taking an action. *So that* is often followed by a verb with *can/could* or *will/would*.
  *I went to the shop **for** some bread. You can use this application **for** editing your photos.*
  *Dolphins come to the surface **in order to** breathe. I locked the cupboard **so as to** keep my things safe.*
  *We went to the cinema early **so that** we could get good seats.*
- We use *because (of)*, *due to* and *as a result of* to talk about what caused an action to happen.
  *We had to drive slowly **because** it was foggy. They've closed the airport **because of** the fog.*
  *Delays are expected **due to** an accident on the M1. The engine stopped **as a result of** overheating.*
- We use *so* or *therefore* to talk about the result of an action.
  *She's had her hair cut very short, **so** she looks quite different now.*
  *Global temperatures are rising. **Therefore** sea levels will also rise.*

Grammar practice

12 Expressing contrast

Circle the correct words.

1 I'm used to living here now, ***despite / although*** I was very homesick at first.
2 Teresa gets very nervous before exams, even ***though / although*** she usually gets good results.
3 ***Despite / In spite*** of the warning signs, they went swimming in the river.
4 ***Even though / In spite*** Phil and Tony are brothers, they have completely different personalities.
5 Despite ***having / he had*** an injured hand, Daniel won the tennis tournament.
6 We really enjoyed the hockey match in spite ***of the rain / that it was raining***.
7 He's determined to buy one of those motorbikes, despite ***that / the fact that*** they're expensive.
8 ***Though / Although*** Ellie and I used to be good friends, we haven't kept in touch since she moved.

13 Reflexive pronouns and *each other*

Complete the dialogues with a relative pronoun or *each other*.

A: Sara's teaching [1] .... to speak Russian.
B: Wow, that's impressive. I could never do that by [2] ....

A: Oh, it's you, Tim. I thought it was George at first. You two look a lot like [3] ....
B: Yes, everyone says that. But when I look at [4] .... in the mirror, I can't really see the similarity.

A: Are we allowed to discuss these questions with [5] .... ?
B: No, I'd like you to work out the answers for [6] ....

A: This photo must be ten years old. Can you recognise [7] .... there?
B: Oh yes! That was at the theme park. We all enjoyed [8] .... that day.
A: Except for Alex. He ate too much and made [9] .... sick.

14 Expressions of purpose, reason and result

Complete the sentences so that the meaning is the same. Use the word in brackets.

1 I wanted to check my emails, so I went online. (to)
I went online ....
2 Because of the flood, many homes were damaged. (result)
Many homes ....
3 He's taken a second job so that he can earn some extra money. (order)
He's taken ....
4 That cable is used to connect the camera to the computer. (for)
That cable ....
5 The river is polluted; therefore the water is unsafe to drink. (due)
The water is ....

15 Passive review

Present simple passive							
It	**'s (is)**	**made**	of plastic.	It	**isn't**	**made**	of plastic.
They	**'re (are)**	**written**	in English.	They	**aren't**	**written**	in English.
Is	it	**made**	of plastic?	Yes, it **is**.		No, it **isn't**.	
Are	they	**written**	in English?	Yes, they **are**.		No, they **aren't**.	

- In a passive sentence the subject doesn't do the action. It is the 'receiver' of the action, which is done by something/someone else.

  Active
  They produce this cheese in France.
  Someone stole two paintings last night.

  Passive
  *This cheese **is produced** in France.*
  *Two paintings **were stolen** last night.*

- We often use the passive when we don't know who/what does the action, or when it isn't important to identify them. If we want to say who/what does the action, we use *by*.

  *The building was designed **by** Gaudí.* *Damage is often caused **by** storms.*

- We form passives with the verb *be* + past participle.
- Most tenses have a passive form. To make a present simple verb passive, we use the present simple form of *be*; for the past simple passive, we use the past simple form of *be*, and so on.

  Past simple: *When **was** that album **recorded**?*
  Present continuous: *Plans **are being made** for a new concert hall.*
  Past continuous: *We couldn't go along West Street because the road **was being repaired**.*
  Present perfect: *Lots of books **have been written** on this subject.*
  Past perfect: *By Monday morning, all the tickets **had been sold**.*

- We can also use modal verbs + *be* + past participle.

  *My new desk **will be delivered** next week.*
  *More details **can be found** on our website.*
  *Computers **must be switched** off while the plane is landing.*
  *The dish **should be cooked** for about an hour.*

16 *have/get* something done

*My parents are going to **have** the house **painted**.*
*Have you **had** your television **repaired** yet?*
*I want to **get** my hair **dyed** black.*
*They **got** an extra room **built** on their house.*

- We use *have/get* + object + past participle when we arrange for someone else to do a service for us.
- If we want to identify the person doing the service, we use *by*.

  *They had/got their wedding photos taken **by** a professional photographer.*

Grammar practice

15 Passive review

a Rewrite the sentences in the passive.

1 They served the dish with chips and salad. ....

2 They haven't solved the problem yet. ....

3 What do people use those machines for? ....

4 People must not ride skateboards here. ....

5 When did someone write that novel? ....

6 Three judges will choose the winner. ....

b Complete the dialogue and the text with passive verbs.

A: My old laptop [1] .... (take) away this morning with all the other stuff for recycling. I was quite sad to see it go.

B: [2] .... your new computer .... (deliver) yet?

A: Not yet, but I've had an email, so I know the order [3] .... (receive) yesterday. Things [4] .... usually .... (send) out straight away, so it might get here this afternoon.

Tea [5] .... (drink) in England since the 17th century, when it [6] .... (bring) here from India, and it's still our favourite drink. This particular black tea [7] .... (grow) in the Darjeeling area and it's my personal favourite. It [8] .... (not supply) by supermarkets, but you'll find it in shops where special types of tea [9] .... (sell), or it [10] .... (can / order) on the internet.

16 *have/get* something done

Complete the sentences. Use the words in brackets in the correct order and the correct form.

1 She always .... at the Redwood Salon. (her hair – have / cut)

2 He'll have to .... at the garage. (his car – get / repair)

3 They .... at the moment. (their garden – have / redesign)

4 The dress was too large, so I .... (it – have / alter)

5 You can .... in that shop. (piercings – get / do)

6 Mum .... for my sister's 21st birthday last month. (special cake – get / make)

17 Conditionals

First conditional

If *I* ***see*** *Carla,* ***I'll tell*** *her to call you.*
If *it* ***doesn't rain****, we'****ll play*** *tennis this afternoon.*
Dave ***will come*** *round later* ***if*** *he* ***has*** *time.*
What ***will*** *you* ***do if*** *you* ***can't*** *get a job?*

- We use the first conditional to talk about possible situations in the future. The action depends on a condition that is possible but not certain.
- Instead of *if* + *not*, we can use *unless*.

If *it* ***doesn't rain****,* ***Unless*** *it* ***rains****,*	*we'll play tennis this afternoon.*

- In the result clause, we can use *might* or *may* instead of *will* if we are more uncertain about the result.
  Dave ***might/may*** *come round later if he has time.*

Second conditional

If *I* ***won*** *lots of money, I'****d travel*** *round the world.*
If *the air* ***didn't contain*** *oxygen, we* ***wouldn't be*** *able to survive.*
More people ***would buy*** *these products* ***if*** *they* ***weren't*** *so expensive.*
Where ***would*** *you* ***live if*** *you* ***could*** *choose any place in the world?*

- We use the second conditional when we are imagining an unreal situation now or in the future. The action depends on a condition that is unlikely or impossible.
- When the verb in the *if* clause is *be*, we sometimes use *I/he/she/it* ***were*** instead of *was*. This is usual when the subject is *I*. With *he/she/it* this form is less commonly used.
  If I ***were*** *you, I'd see a doctor.* (**not** ~~*was*~~)
  We'd have lunch in the garden if it ***wasn't / weren't*** *so windy.*
- In the result clause, we can use *might* instead of *would* if we are more uncertain about the result. We can use *could* to mean 'would be able to'.
  More people ***might*** *buy these products if they weren't so expensive.*
  If the air didn't contain oxygen, we ***couldn't*** *survive.*

Third conditional

If Lisa ***had needed*** *help, she* ***would have called*** *us.* (But she didn't need help, so she didn't call.)
If *they* ***hadn't*** *invited us, we* ***wouldn't have come****.* (But they did invite us, so we came.)
I ***wouldn't have failed*** *the test* ***if*** *I'****d studied*** *for it.* (But I didn't study for it, so I failed.)
What ***would*** *you* ***have done if*** *we* ***hadn't been*** *here?*

- We use the third conditional when we are imagining a situation in the past that did not happen in reality. The action depends on a condition that is impossible because the past can't be changed.
- In the result clause, we can use *might have* or *may have* instead of *would have* if we are more uncertain about the result. We can use *could have* to mean 'would have been able to'.
  If we hadn't played so badly, we ***might/may*** *have won.*
  If Lisa had needed help, she ***could have*** *called us.*

Grammar practice

17 Conditionals

a Match the two parts of the sentences.

1 If Paul doesn't do well in his exams, ☐
2 If we reorganised the room, ☐
3 It would be a great achievement if ☐
4 We'll have to leave without him if ☐
5 If he wasn't so lazy, ☐
6 If we can't get in touch with Adam, ☐
7 People won't know about the event unless ☐
8 He'd get a new surfboard if ☐

A he'd give us a hand with the cleaning.
B he could afford it.
C we publicise it.
D he managed to break the record.
E he'll be very disappointed.
F he doesn't come soon.
G it might look better.
H he won't know where to meet us.

b Complete the third conditional sentences with the correct form of the verbs.

A: Those red shoes were lovely! I [1] .... (try) them on if I [2] .... (be) able to afford them.
B: Well, you [3] .... (can / buy) them if you [4] .... (not spend) all your money on computer games.

A: What a depressing result!
B: Of course, they [5] .... (play) better if the ground [6] .... (not be) so muddy.
A: And if Palmer [7] .... (not miss) that goal in the first half, everything [8] .... (might be) different.

c Choose the correct answer: A, B or C.

1 You would have known what to do if .... the instructions properly.
A you read **B** you'd read **C** you'll read
2 If the bus .... on time, we'll get to the cinema in about 20 minutes.
A is **B** was **C** will be
3 If Eva had been more confident in the interview, she .... have got the job.
A will **B** can **C** might
4 The accident .... have happened if they had stopped at the lights.
A won't **B** wouldn't **C** didn't
5 I'd report this to the police if .... you.
A I was **B** I were **C** I'd been
6 If I .... run out of money, I could have gone to the café for a pizza.
A hadn't **B** didn't **C** wouldn't have
7 What will you do if this situation .... ?
A doesn't improve **B** didn't improve **C** hadn't improved
8 If he didn't keep losing his temper, he .... so hard to get on with.
A wasn't **B** hadn't been **C** wouldn't be

Grammar reference

18 *should, ought to, had better* and *it's time*

- We use *should* or *ought to* + infinitive to give advice or to say what we believe is right or appropriate.
  *You **should try** to finish your essay before you go out.*
  *People **shouldn't care** so much about money.*
  *It's a good film. You **ought to go** and see it.*
  *We **ought to be** able to trust our politicians.*
- The usual negative form is *shouldn't*. *Ought not to* is also correct, but it isn't commonly used.
- We use *had better* + infinitive to give advice, often as a warning. We mean that if the action isn't taken, a negative result is likely to follow.
  *It's getting late. I**'d better go** now.*
  *You**'d better get** up at 6:30 if you want to catch the early train.*
  *We**'d better not leave** our bags here. They might get stolen.*
- The negative form is *had better not*.
- We use *It's time* + past simple when we want to criticise someone's present behaviour.
  ***It's time** she **cleaned** up her room. It looks awful!*
  ***It's time** he **learned** how to cook.*
- There is no negative form for this structure.
  ***It's time** you **stopped** wasting money.* (**not** ~~*It isn't time you wasted*~~ or ~~*It's time you didn't waste*~~)

19 Expressing wishes and regrets

wish and *if only*

- We use *wish* and *if only* when we want something to be true, even though it is unlikely or impossible. *If only* is similar to *I wish*, but stronger.
- We use *wish / if only* + past simple when we want a present situation to be different but can't change it.
  *I wish we **lived** in New York.* (But the reality is that we don't live there.)
  *If only the tickets **didn't cost** so much!* (But they do cost a lot.)
- We use *wish / if only* + *would* + infinitive when we would like something/someone else to take action now or in the future. We have no power to make this happen.
  *If only Leo **would change** his mind!* (It's possible but unlikely that he will do this.)
  *I wish my sisters **wouldn't argue** all the time.* (They could stop doing this, but they probably won't.)
- We use *wish / if only* + past perfect to express regret about an action or situation in the past.
  *I wish **I'd brought** a jumper with me.* (But I didn't bring one and the past can't be changed.)
  *If only it **hadn't been** so cold!* (But it was cold.)

should have

- We use *should have* + past participle to express regret or to criticise someone's behaviour in the past.
  *There aren't any seats left. We **should have got** here earlier.*
  *I didn't know about Renata's illness. You **should have told** me.*
  *Sorry – I **shouldn't have said** that. It was a stupid thing to say.*
  *She **shouldn't have embarrassed** Ben in front of his friends.*

Grammar practice

18 *should*, *ought to*, *had better* and *it's time*

a Match the two parts of the sentences.

1 You should	☐	**A** be so expensive.
2 I think you ought	☐	**B** try to see my point of view.
3 I'd better	☐	**C** go swimming here – it might not be safe.
4 These phones shouldn't	☐	**D** stopped behaving like a child.
5 It's time Richard	☐	**E** to see a doctor about your shoulder.
6 We'd better not	☐	**F** take an umbrella with me.

b Tick (✓) the correct sentences. If there is a mistake, ~~cross out~~ the wrong word(s) and write the correct word(s).

1 They shouldn't go in there without permission. ....

2 It's time you'd stop blaming other people for your mistakes. ....

3 She better start concentrating more on her work. ....

4 People ought to support this charity. ....

5 Should we try to get some help to solve this problem? ....

6 I hadn't better stay out late tonight. ....

19 Expressing wishes and regrets

a Circle the correct words.

1 I wish Lily *came* / *would come*. We've been waiting here for 15 minutes now.

2 Our neighbours are always watching us. If only they *weren't* / *aren't* so nosy!

3 The sauce isn't very nice. You shouldn't *of* / *have* put in so much salt.

4 We won't be able to get everything before the shops close. If only *we'll have* / *we had* more time!

5 Everyone says it was a brilliant party. I wish *I was* / *I'd been* there.

6 Are you still here? You should *leave* / *have left* ten minutes ago!

7 I'd love to go swimming. If only I *didn't* / *wouldn't* have so much homework to do!

8 I wish we *didn't forget* / *hadn't forgotten* Maria's birthday.

b Complete the text with the correct form of the verbs.

Hi Sal

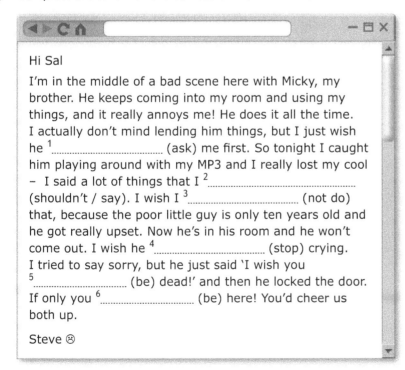

I'm in the middle of a bad scene here with Micky, my brother. He keeps coming into my room and using my things, and it really annoys me! He does it all the time. I actually don't mind lending him things, but I just wish he [1] .... (ask) me first. So tonight I caught him playing around with my MP3 and I really lost my cool – I said a lot of things that I [2] .... (shouldn't / say). I wish I [3] .... (not do) that, because the poor little guy is only ten years old and he got really upset. Now he's in his room and he won't come out. I wish he [4] .... (stop) crying. I tried to say sorry, but he just said 'I wish you [5] .... (be) dead!' and then he locked the door. If only you [6] .... (be) here! You'd cheer us both up.

Steve ☹

20 Participle clauses

- Present participles are the *-ing* form of the verb.
- Past participles usually have the same form as the past simple.
- Perfect participles are formed by *having* + past participle.

✱ For irregular past participles, see page 102.

Connecting two actions

- A clause starting with a present participle often describes something happening at the same time as the main action or just before it.
  ***Walking** to school*, *we often see Kate on her way to work.*
  He came inside, ***carrying the baby in his arms***.
  Grabbing my bag, *I ran out into the street.*
- We can also use a present participle with some conjunctions (e.g. *while*, *before*, *after*) and prepositions (e.g. *by*, *without*, *instead of*).
  While driving back from London, *she ran out of petrol.*
  After working hard all week, *we were glad to relax at the weekend.*
  They searched for an hour ***without finding anything***.

✱ We can also start a clause with a past participle. Here the meaning is passive.
Served with cream, *this cake makes a delicious dessert.*
Written in 1998, *the novel was an instant best-seller.*

- A clause starting with a perfect participle describes something happening before the main action.
  Having spent all her money, *Jane couldn't afford to eat out.*
  Having crossed the bridge, *you should take the first street on the right.*
  He's watching television now, ***having finished his homework***.
- In this type of sentence the participle clause and the main clause must have the same subject.
  Looking *at Sofia,* ~~*she was*~~ *upset.*
  Looking *at Sofia,* ***I could see*** *she was upset.*
  Having seen *the film before,* ~~*it wasn't*~~ *so exciting this time.*
  Having seen *the film before,* ***we didn't find*** *it so exciting this time.*

Acting as a relative clause

- A clause with a present or past participle can also be used instead of a relative clause to give information about a noun.

✱ For relative clauses, see page 100.

- The present participle is active and is used for continuous actions.
  Can you hear that bird ***singing outside***? (= which is singing)
  I noticed two men ***coming out of the building***. (= who were coming)
  The girl ***talking to David*** *is my cousin Sara.* (= who is talking)
- The past participle is passive.
  Tickets ***bought online*** *cost €45.* (= which are bought)
  Our next-door neighbour is a man ***called Mr Johnson***. (= who is called)
  The Eiffel Tower, ***built in 1889***, *is a symbol of France.* (= which was built)

Grammar practice

20 Participle clauses

a Read the sentences. Are the following statements *right* (✓) or *wrong* (✗)?

1 *Looking through the window, I saw three people in the room.*
Three people were looking through the window. ☐

2 *Having read the book, I knew how the film would end.*
I read the book before I saw the film. ☐

3 *Walking through the park yesterday, I found a £5 note.*
The money was in the park. ☐

4 *Nicholas couldn't call Petra, having forgotten her number.*
Petra couldn't remember her phone number. ☐

5 *We could see the bus coming round the corner.*
The bus is coming round the corner now. ☐

6 *The clothes sold in this shop are very cheap.*
This shop sells very cheap clothes. ☐

b Complete the sentences with the correct participle.

1 .... (leave) my watch at home, I didn't know what time it was.
2 .... (work) as a waitress, she has to deal with all sorts of people.
3 They live in a house .... (build) in the 18th century.
4 .... (book) early, they had good seats near the stage.
5 You should make sure the walls are clean before .... (paint) them.
6 .... (have) a big breakfast, we weren't very hungry at lunch time.
7 It's a film .... (star) Harrison Ford and .... (direct) by Steven Spielberg.
8 The novel, ... (write) in the 1950s, tells the story of a boy .... (grow) up in Ireland.

c Complete the sentences with participle clauses, using the words in brackets.

1 .... (miss / their train), they were lucky to find a taxi .... (wait / at the station).

2 .... (sit / alone on the beach), I watched the sun .... (rise / over the ocean).

3 .... (read / the menu), she ordered a chicken dish .... (cook / with

4 This photo, ... (take / last year), shows our garden .... (cover / with snow).

21 Modals of deduction and possibility review

Not sure					
I He We	**might** **may** **could**	**be** in the team. **arrive** soon. **have seen** this film.	I He We	**might not** **may not**	**be** in the team. **arrive** soon. **have seen** this film.
Sure					
She You They	**must**	**be** Spanish. **arrive** soon. **have seen** this film.	She You They	**can't** **couldn't**	**be** Spanish. **have seen** this film.

- We use modal verbs + infinitive to talk about possibilities in the present or future.
- We use *might*, *may* or *could* when we think something is possibly true, but we aren't sure. For the negative we use *might not* or *may not* (but not *could not*).
  A: Who's that girl? B: I don't know. She ***might/may/could be*** *Matthew's sister.*
  I'll try to see you before you leave, but I ***might/may not get*** *there in time.* **(not** ~~could not get~~**)**
- We use *must* when we feel sure that something is true. We use *can't* or *couldn't*, usually followed by the verb *be*, when we feel sure that something is not true.
  They left the gym half an hour ago, so they ***must get*** *home soon.*
  He ***can't/couldn't be*** *in Madrid. He told me he was going to Switzerland.* **(not** ~~He mustn't be~~**)**
- We use the same modal verbs + *have* + past participle to talk about possibilities in the past.
  I'm a bit worried – I ***might have forgotten*** *to lock the back door before I left.*
  It's probably too early to ring Simon. He ***may not have woken*** *up yet.*
  Clare was sitting right in front of us. You ***must have seen*** *her!*
  I'm sure their story was true. They ***can't/couldn't have made*** *it up.*

22 Question tag review

Positive statement	Question tag	Negative statement	Question tag
I**'m** in the team,	**aren't** I?	I**'m not** a great singer,	**am** I?
He **was** surprised,	**wasn't** he?	She **wasn't** unhappy,	**was** she?
You**'re** working,	**aren't** you?	You **aren't** listening,	**are** you?
She**'s** gone home,	**hasn't** she?	He **hasn't** left,	**has** he?
It**'ll** be fun,	**won't** it?	It **won't** rain,	**will** it?
They **can** fly,	**can't** they?	They **can't** see us,	**can** they?
I **should** leave,	**shouldn't** I?	I **shouldn't** be here,	**should** I?
She wears glasses,	**doesn't** she?	He **doesn't** drive,	**does** he?
You went out,	**didn't** you?	You **didn't** see me,	**did** you?

- We add a question tag to a statement to check information or to invite agreement.
- If the main verb is positive, the question tag is negative. If it is negative, the question tag is positive.
- When the main verb is *be*, we repeat the verb *be* in the question tag.
- For other verb forms, we repeat the auxiliary or modal in the question tag. For a present or past simple positive verb, where there is no auxiliary or modal, we use *don't/doesn't* or *didn't*.
- We can add a question tag to an imperative to make a request. We use *will*, *would* or *can* + *you*.
  Put *this bowl on the table,* ***will you?*** *Take out the rubbish,* ***would you?*** *Give me a hand,* ***ca***

Grammar practice

21 Modals of deduction and possibility review

a Complete the sentences with modal verbs. Sometimes there is more than one possible answer.

1 A: I've been studying all afternoon.
B: Yes, I know. You .... be tired.

2 A: What are you doing on Saturday?
B: I'm not sure yet. We .... go skiing.

3 A: I think I saw Rosa going into the stadium.
B: No, it .... have been her. She and her family have gone away this weekend.

4 A: You'll come shopping with me, won't you?
B: I'll try, but I .... not have time.

5 A: Can't you find your glasses?
B: No! I .... have left them at home.

6 A: Where's Lee? You rang him, didn't you?
B: Yes, but I suppose he .... not have got my message.

b Rewrite the sentences so that the meaning is the same. Use the word in brackets.

1 It's possible that Joanna will win the competition. (could)

....

2 I'm certain that this box weighs more than two kilos. (must)

....

3 Perhaps they went to the shopping centre. (may)

....

4 Maybe you won't enjoy this song. (might)

....

5 Those men definitely weren't police officers – I'm sure of that. (can't)

....

6 I'm convinced that she wrote the lyrics for that song. (must)

....

22 Question tag review

a Match the two parts of the sentences.

1 Sara's got a new job,	☐	**A**	will she?
2 She won't persuade Philip to come,	☐	**B**	should she?
3 Petra lives in Manchester,	☐	**C**	didn't she?
4 She's not a member of staff,	☐	**D**	hasn't she?
5 Diana shouldn't be upset,	☐	**E**	is she?
6 She really lost her temper,	☐	**F**	doesn't she?

b Complete the sentences with question tags.

1 People weren't very impressed by his latest film, ... ?
2 The campaign hasn't succeeded in raising much money, ... ?
3 They went on a training course last month, ... ?
4 Your brother would like to be a computer programmer, ... ?
5 You won't mention this to anyone else, ... ?
6 If I give the wrong answer, I'm going to look stupid, ... ?

23 Reported speech review

Direct speech	Reported speech	
'I **want** to have an ice cream.' 'The TV **isn't working**.' 'My results **have improved**.' 'Someone **stole** my wallet.' 'The exhibition **will** be interesting.' 'I **can't** remember my password.'	Tom said (that) Tom told me (that)	he **wanted** to have an ice cream. the TV **wasn't working**. his results **had improved**. someone had **stolen** his wallet. the exhibition **would** be interesting. he **couldn't** remember his password.
'When **are** they **arriving**?' 'Who **did** you **speak** to?' '**Are** you **learning** English?' '**Has** Alice **called**?'	Julia asked (me)	when they **were arriving**. who I **had spoken** to. **if/whether** I **was learning** English. **if/whether** Alice **had called**.
'**Stop** complaining!' '**Don't take** photos in the gallery.'	He told me	**to stop** complaining. **not to take** photos in the gallery.

- When we report a statement or a question, we usually change the tense. The verb usually moves 'one step back' into the past: present > past, past > past perfect, *will* > *would*, *can* > *could*.
- However, when reporting something that remains true, we don't need to change the tense.
  'I like living in Prague.' *She said she* ***likes/liked*** *living in Prague.*
  'Toledo is a city in Spain.' *He told me Toledo* ***is/was*** *a city in Spain.*
  'Napoleon died in 1821.' *She said that Napoleon* ***died/had died*** *in 1821.*
- When we report a question, we change the word order to the form of a statement. For an information question, we repeat the question word. For a *yes/no* question, we use *if* or *whether*.
- For a command, the reporting verb is usually *tell*. The form is *tell* someone (*not*) *to* + infinitive.
- Pronouns and possessive adjectives may need to change in reported speech.
  *'**I** rang **you** on **your** mobile.'* *Annie told me **she** had rung **me** on **my** mobile.*

24 Reporting verbs

- Most reporting verbs are followed by *that* + a full clause in reported speech.
  He mentioned / explained / complained / announced / reported / replied ***that*** *the concert had been delayed.*
- The verbs *admit*, *deny*, *recommend* and *suggest* can also be followed by a verb with *-ing*.
  She admitted / denied ***taking / that she had taken*** *the money.*
  They recommended / suggested ***trying / that we try*** *their new product.*

✱ For other verbs followed by *-ing* or the infinitive, see page 82.

- The verbs *agree*, *offer*, *promise* and *refuse* are followed by *to* + infinitive.
  I agreed / offered / promised / refused ***to lend*** *him the money.*
- These verbs are followed by *to* + object (person) + infinitive: *advise*, *ask*, *convince*, *encourage*, *invite*, *order*, *persuade*, *tell*, *warn*. Some of these can also be followed by object + *that* clause.
  She advised / asked / encouraged / invited / ordered ***us to tell*** *the truth.*
  He convinced / persuaded / told / warned ***them to stop*** / ***them that they should stop*** *smoking.*
- For verbs with the infinitive, notice the difference between these negative forms.
  I didn't promise to come. (= I didn't make this promise.) *I promised not to come.* (= I said, 'I won't come.')
  She won't persuade him to buy it. (= She won't manage to persuade him.)
  She'll persuade him not to buy it. (= He won't buy it because of her persuasion.)

Grammar practice

23 Reported speech review

Read the dialogue and complete the reported speech.

Mike: I've decided to go to the science museum later. Do you want to come?
Hana: Why are you going there? Walking round a museum doesn't sound like fun.
Mike: Have you ever been there?
Hana: No.
Mike: Well, it's brilliant. They've created hundreds of interactive exhibits, so it isn't like an old-fashioned museum. Come with me! You won't regret it.
Hana: OK, then. I'll come.

Mike said that [1] .... and asked Hana [2] .... Hana asked [3] .... and said that [4] .... Mike asked her [5] .... When she said no, he told her that it [6] .... He explained that [7] .... , so it [8] .... He encouraged her to come with him and said [9] .... , so finally Hana agreed to come.

24 Reporting verbs

a Circle the correct words.

1 Sam tried to persuade *me to come / that I'd come*.
2 She complained *to be / that she was* too hot.
3 Do you recommend *seeing / people to see* this film?
4 They ordered us *to not / not to* leave the room.
5 She denies *breaking / to break* into the house.
6 He offered *to buy / that he would buy* me a coffee.

b Read the dialogues and complete the sentences.

1 **Danny:** Did you get angry?
Keith: Yes, I did.
Keith admitted ....

2 **Rachel:** Please don't tell anybody.
Katerina: OK, I won't.
Katerina promised ....

3 **Sania:** What should I do?
Ahmed: I think you should tell your parents.
Ahmed advised ....

4 **Matthew:** I expected to see Julie here.
Nadia: No, she's practising for the play.
Nadia explained ....

5 **Sofia:** I'd like to go out somewhere tomorrow.
Luke: OK, let's go to the cinema.
Luke suggested ....

6 **Diego:** It's no good – I can't do this.
Martin: Come on, don't give up!
Martin encouraged ....

25 Relative clause review

Defining relative clauses

I know lots of people ***who/that come from Scotland****.*
Jack is someone ***whose jokes always make me laugh****.*
The bus ***that/which goes along King Street*** *will take you to the station.*
The shop ***where Lara works*** *isn't open on Sundays.*

- A relative clause refers to someone or something earlier in the sentence.
- A defining relative clause gives essential information – we need it to identify the person/thing we are talking about.
- We normally use *who* for people, but we can also use *that*.
  It was Tony ***who/that*** *persuaded me to enter the competition.*
- We use *whose* for people when we want to talk about something that belongs to them. *Whose* is a possessive form which we use instead of *his*, *her* or *their*. It is always followed by a noun.
  We've never met the woman ***whose*** *flat is above ours.*
- We use *that* or *which* for things.
  These are the gloves ***that/which*** *I bought for Mum's birthday.*
- We use *where* for places. It means 'in which', 'at which' or 'to which' and it is followed by a noun or pronoun.
  Málaga is the city ***where*** *Picasso was born.* (*where* = in which)
  Did they like the hotel ***where*** *they were staying?* (*where* = at which)
  The café ***where*** *we used to go has been sold.* (*where* = to which)
- In a defining relative clause, we can often leave out *who*, *which* or *that* when it is the object of the verb.
  She's someone we met at Sam's party. (= who/that we met)
  Did you get the postcard I sent you? (= that/which I sent you)

Non-defining relative clauses

At the market I bumped into Paula, ***who was on her way to the gym****.*
The woman at the bank, ***whose name I've forgotten now****, was very helpful.*
They're building a new theatre, ***which should be finished by the end of the year****.*
Bari, ***where Stefano grew up****, is in the south of Italy.*

- A non-defining relative clause is not essential but adds extra information. It is separated from the rest of the sentence by commas.
- The pronouns are mostly the same as in defining relative clauses. However, in non-defining clauses we don't use the pronoun *that*.
  I was staying with my aunt, ***who*** *lives in a village near Bristol.* (**not** *my aunt, ~~that~~ …*)
  The film, ***which*** *was directed by Tom Hooper, was released in 2011.* (**not** *The film, ~~that~~ …*)

Grammar practice

25 Relative clause review

a Underline the relative clause and circle the correct pronoun.

Defining relative clauses

1 The charity concert *where / that* they organised raised over £5,000.
2 This is a website *where / which* you'll find lots of information.
3 I don't know anyone *who / whose* birthday is the same as mine.
4 A lot of people *who / where* come from Canada speak both French and English.

Non-defining relative clauses

5 Duke Street, *which / where* Jessica lives, is on the other side of the park.
6 I've just been visiting my grandmother, *who / that* is in hospital.
7 The police were interviewing Mr Clark, *who / whose* car was stolen last night.
8 The world's smallest bird, *that / which* lives in Cuba, is only 5 cm long.

b Tick the sentence in *italics* if it is correct. If there is a mistake, ~~cross out~~ the wrong word(s) and write the correct word(s).

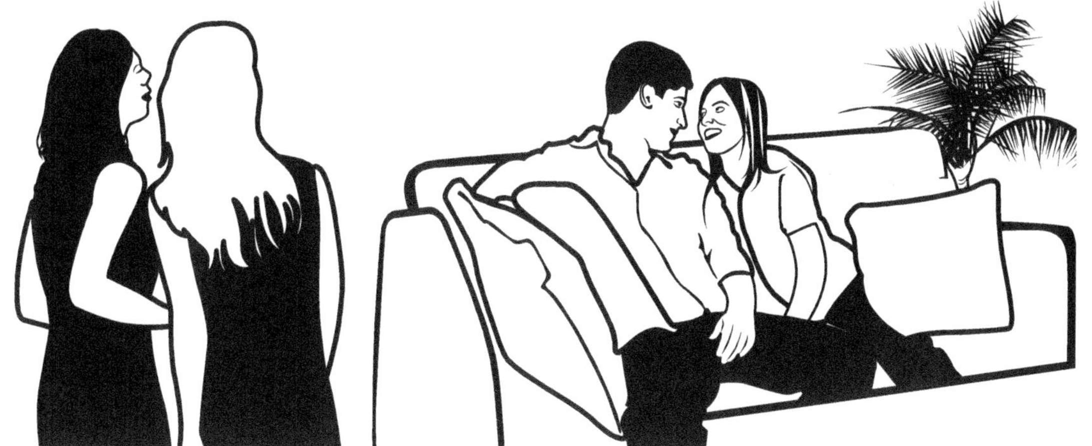

A: I can see Evan over there. How is he?
B: Great. [1]*He's found a really nice girlfriend, who her name is Emily.* Everyone in the family is pleased. [2]*It looks like this might be a relationship that will last for a while.*
A: [3]*Is Emily the girl whose sitting next to him?*
B: Yes, that's right. [4]*They met at the Olive Tree, which is a café in Portman Street.* [5]*It's a place which Evan often goes because it's close to his office.*
A: Oh yes, I know it. [6]*My dad, who loves Greek food used to take us there sometimes.* [7]*I especially remember the bread, that was absolutely delicious.*

1 ....
2 ....
3 ....
4 ....
5 ....
6 ....
7 ....

c Join the two sentences using a relative clause.

1 That building on the corner is the National Bank. Pete's mother works there.

....

2 For lunch I had a mushroom omelette. It was served with salad.

....

3 The shirt was a present from Helen. Alex is wearing it.

....

4 Can you remember the name of the actor? He starred in *Psycho*.

....

5 I got a lift to the station with Fiona. Her boyfriend has a car.

....

Irregular verbs

Verb	Past simple	Past participle	Verb	Past simple	Past participle
be	was/were	been	lose	lost	lost
become	became	become	make	made	made
begin	began	begun	mean	meant	meant
blow	blew	blown	meet	met	met
break	broke	broken	pay	paid	paid
bring	brought	brought	put	put	put
build	built	built	read	read	read
burn	burned/burnt	burned/burnt	ride	rode	ridden
buy	bought	bought	ring	rang	rung
can	could	been able	run	ran	run
catch	caught	caught	say	said	said
choose	chose	chosen	see	saw	seen
come	came	come	sell	sold	sold
cost	cost	cost	send	sent	sent
cut	cut	cut	set	set	set
do	did	done	shake	shook	shaken
draw	drew	drawn	shoot	shot	shot
drink	drank	drunk	shut	shut	shut
drive	drove	driven	sing	sang	sung
eat	ate	eaten	sit	sat	sat
fall	fell	fallen	sleep	slept	slept
feel	felt	felt	speak	spoke	spoken
fight	fought	fought	spell	spelled/spelt	spelled/spelt
find	found	found	spend	spent	spent
fly	flew	flown	spin	span/spun	spun
forget	forgot	forgotten	stand	stood	stood
get	got	got	steal	stole	stolen
give	gave	given	strike	struck	struck
go	went	gone/been	swim	swam	swum
grow	grew	grown	swing	swung	swung
have	had	had	take	took	taken
hear	heard	heard	teach	taught	taught
hit	hit	hit	tell	told	told
hold	held	held	think	thought	thought
hurt	hurt	hurt	throw	threw	thrown
keep	kept	kept	understand	understood	understood
know	knew	known	wake	woke	woken
learn	learned/learnt	learned/learnt	wear	wore	worn
leave	left	left	win	won	won
lend	lent	lent	write	wrote	written
let	let	let			

Phonemic chart

Consonant sounds

/b/ bird

/tʃ/ cheese

/d/ door

/f/ fish

/g/ girl

/h/ heart

/dʒ/ jam

/k/ key

/l/ leaf

/m/ monkey

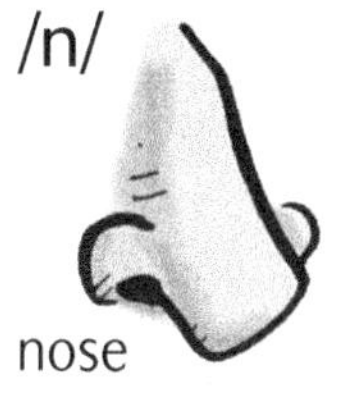
/n/ nose

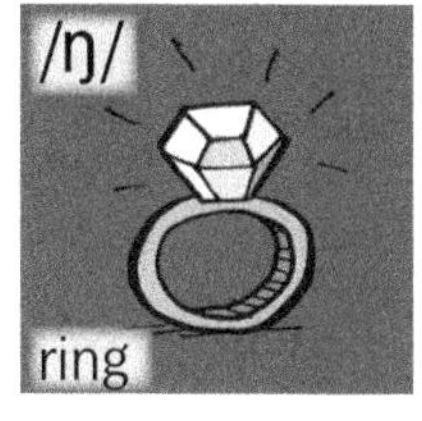
/ŋ/ ring

/p/ pen

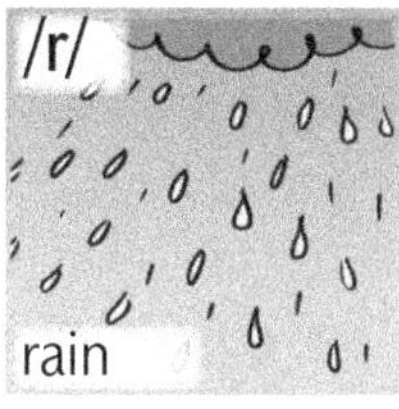
/r/ rain

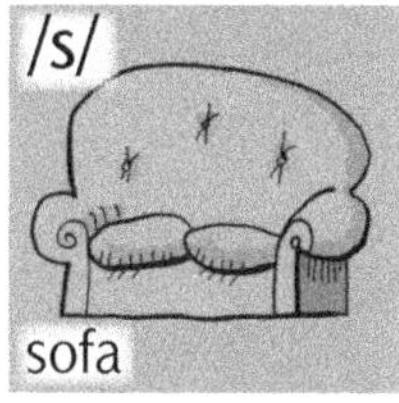
/s/ sofa

/ʃ/ shoe

/ʒ/ television

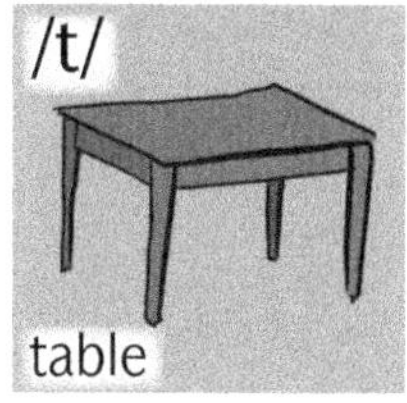
/t/ table

/ð/ feather

/θ/ think

/v/ volcano

/w/ window

/j/ yoga

/z/ zoo

Vowel sounds

/æ/ apple

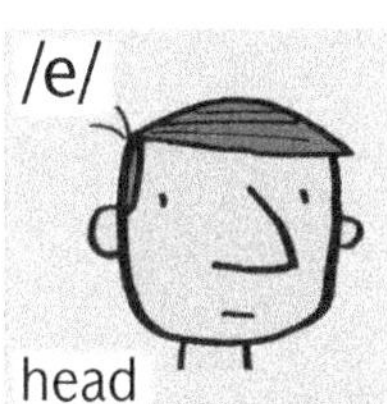
/e/ head

/ɪ/ insect

/ɒ/ hot

/ʌ/ umbrella

/ʊ/ book

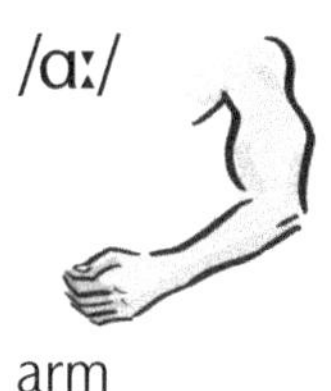
/ɑː/ arm

/ɜː/ earth

/iː/ sheep

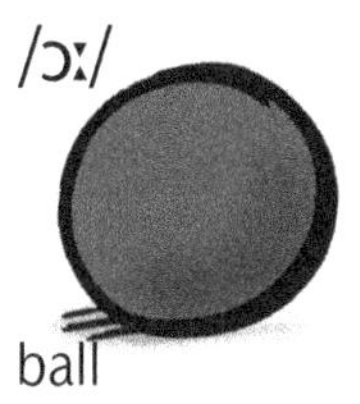
/ɔː/ ball

/uː/ moon

/eə/ chair

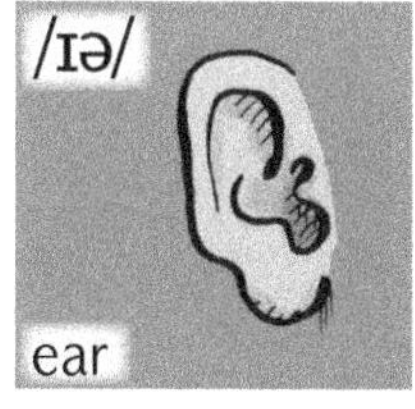
/ɪə/ ear

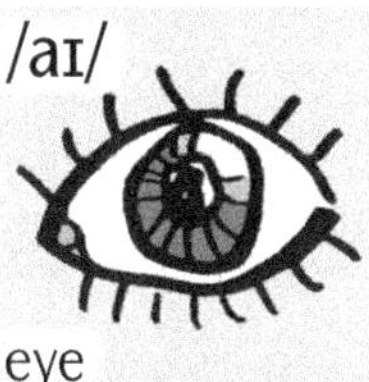
/aɪ/ eye

/eɪ/ paper

/ɔɪ/ boy

/əʊ/ phone

/aʊ/ owl

/ə/ computer

Go to the Interactive website to download the workbook audio.

www.cambridge.org/interactive